KU-620-690

ARSENIC AND OLD LACE

WITHDRAWN

LIVERPOOL JMU LIBRARY

3 1111 01510 5826

WITHDRAWN

ARSENIC AND OLD LACE

by Joseph Kesselring

JOSEF WEINBERGER PLAYS

LONDON

First published in the United Kingdom in 1948 by
Josef Weinberger Ltd (pka English Theatre Guild Ltd)
12-14 Mortimer Street, London, W1T 3JJ
Second Edition 1986
Reprinted 1988, 1994, 1998, 2001

Copyright © 1941 by Random House, Inc, USA & Canada
Copyright © 1942 by Dramatists Play Service, Inc.
Copyright renewed 1968 and 1969 by Charlotte Kesselring

ISBN 0 85676 122 2

This play is protected by Copyright. According to Copyright Law, no public
performance or reading of a protected play or part of that play may be given without
prior authorization from Josef Weinberger Plays, as agent for the Copyright Owners.

From time to time it is necessary to restrict or even withdraw the rights of certain
plays. **It is therefore essential to check with us before making a
commitment to produce a play.**

NO PERFORMANCE MAY BE GIVEN WITHOUT A LICENCE

AMATEUR PRODUCTIONS
Royalties are due at least fourteen days prior to the first performance. A royalty
quotation will be issued upon receipt of the following details:

Name of Licensee
Play Title
Place of Performance
Dates and Number of Performances
Audience Capacity
Ticket Prices

PROFESSIONAL PRODUCTIONS
All enquiries regarding professional rights should be addressed to Josef Weinberger
Ltd, 12-14 Mortimer Street, London W1t 3JJ

OVERSEAS PRODUCTIONS
Applications for productions overseas should be addressed to our local authorised
agents. Further details are listed in our catalogue of plays, published every two
years, or available from Josef Weinberger Plays at the address above.

CONDITIONS OF SALE
This book is sold subject to the condition that it shall not by way of trade or
otherwise be resold, hired out, circulated or distributed without prior consent of the
Publisher. **Reproduction of the text either in whole or part and by any
means is strictly forbidden.**

Printed by Commercial Colour Press
Cover design by Robin Lowry

ARSENIC AND OLD LACE was presented by Howard Lindsay and Russel Crouse at the Fulton Theatre in New York, on 18 August 1941, with the following cast:—

ABBY BREWSTER	Josephine Hull
THE REV. DR. HARPER	Wyrley Birch
TEDDY BREWSTER	John Alexander
OFFICER BROPHY	John Quigg
OFFICER KLEIN	Bruce Gordon
MARTHA BREWSTER	Jean Adair
ELAINE HARPER	Helen Brooks
MORTIMER BREWSTER	Allyn Joslyn
MR. GIBBS	Henry Herbert
JONATHAN BREWSTER	Boris Karloff
DR. EINSTEIN	Edgar Stehli
OFFICER O'HARA	Anthony Ross
LIEUTENANT ROONEY	Victor Sutherland
MR. WITHERSPOON	William Parks

This play was presented by Firth Shephard at the Strand Theatre, London, on 23 December 1942, with the following cast:—

ABBY BREWSTER	Lillian Braithwaite
THE REV. DR. HARPER	Clarence Bigge
TEDDY BREWSTER	Frank Pettingell
OFFICER BROPHY	George Dillon
OFFICER KLEIN	E. J. Kennedy
MARTHA BREWSTER	Mary Jerrold
ELAINE HARPER	Eileen Bennett
MORTIMER BREWSTER	Naunton Wayne
MR. GIBBS	Fred Beck
JONATHAN BREWSTER	Edmund Willard
DR. EINSTEIN	Martin Miller
OFFICER O'HARA	Cyril Smith
LIEUTENANT ROONEY	Frank Tilton
MR. WITHERSPOON	Wilfred Caithness

The entire action of the play takes place in the living-room of the Brewster home in Brooklyn. Time: the present

ACT I:	An afternoon in September.	
ACT II:	That same night.	
ACT III:	SCENE I :	Later that night.
	SCENE II:	Early the next morning.

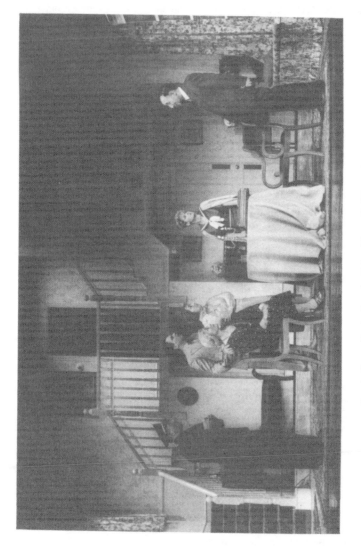

photo by Fergus Bourke from the Gaiety Theatre Dublin production

ACT ONE

TIME: *Late afternoon, September. Present.*
PLACE: *The living-room of the old Brewster home in Brooklyn, N.Y. It is just as Victorian as the two sisters, Abby and Martha Brewster, who occupy the house with their nephew, Teddy.*
There is a staircase* U.R. leading to the upper floor, broken by a landing with a window looking out on the front porch. At the top of the stairs a balcony with a door leading to bedrooms, and an archway beyond which are stairs to the top floor. There is a large window D.L. below which is a long window-seat. There is a door U.C. that leads to the cellar, another to L. of it, that leads to the kitchen, and at R. the main door of the house, which opens on to the porch, D.R (See stage diagram at end of play.)
When the curtain rises, ABBY BREWSTER, *a plump little darling in her late sixties, is presiding at the tea-table. The table is lighted by candles. Seated in armchair at her left is the* REV. DR. HARPER, *and on her right, standing, her nephew,* TEDDY, *whose costume includes a frock coat and pince-nez attached to a black ribbon.* TEDDY *is in his forties and has a large black moustache, and his manner and make-up suggest Theodore Roosevelt.*

ABBY. Yes, indeed, my sister Martha and I have been talking all week about your sermon last Sunday. It's really wonderful, Dr. Harper—in only two short years you've taken on the spirit of Brooklyn.

DR. HARPER. That's very gratifying, Miss Brewster.

ABBY. You see, living here next to the church all our lives, we've seen so many ministers come and go. The spirit of Brooklyn we always say is friendliness—and your sermons are not so much sermons as friendly talks.

TEDDY. Personally, I've always enjoyed my talks with Cardinal Giddons—or have I met him yet?

ABBY. No, dear, not yet. (*Changing the subject.*) Are the biscuits good?

---

* The staircase and landing described here are a necessary part of the set as originally produced. However, in certain theatres it may not be possible to construct a practical staircase and landing; in which case a wide entrance can be substituted for the bottom of the stairs, with perhaps two or three practical steps showing. Some rearrangement of business and lines will, of course, in this case be necessary.

LIVERPOOL JOHN MOORES UNIVERSITY
LEARNING SERVICES

TEDDY (*He sits on sofa*). Bully!

ABBY. Won't you have another biscuit, Dr. Harper?

DR. HARPER. Oh, no, I'm afraid I'll have no appetite for dinner now. I always eat too many of your biscuits just to taste that lovely jam.

ABBY. But you haven't tried the quince. We always put a little apple in with it to take the tartness out.

DR. HARPER. No, thank you.

ABBY. We'll send you over a jar.

DR. HARPER. No, no. You keep it here so I can be sure of having your biscuits with it.

ABBY. I do hope they don't make us use that imitation flour again. I mean with this war trouble. It may not be very charitable of me, but I've almost come to the conclusion that this Mr. Hitler isn't a Christian.

DR. HARPER (*with a sigh*). If only Europe were on another planet!

TEDDY (*sharply*). Europe, sir?

DR. HARPER. Yes, Teddy.

TEDDY. Point your gun the other way!

DR. HARPER. Gun?

ABBY (*trying to calm him*). Teddy.

TEDDY. To the West! There's your danger! There's your enemy! Japan!

DR. HARPER. Why, yes—yes, of course.

ABBY. Teddy!

TEDDY. No, Aunt Abby! Not so much talk about Europe and more about the canal!

ABBY. Well, let's not talk about war. Will you have another cup of tea, dear?

TEDDY. No, thank you, Aunt Abby.

ABBY. Dr. Harper?

DR. HARPER. No, thank you. I must admit, Miss Abby, that war and violence seem far removed from these surroundings.

ABBY. It is peaceful here, isn't it?

DR. HARPER. Yes—peaceful. The virtues of another day—they're all here in this house. The gentle virtues that went out with candlelight and good manners and low taxes.

ABBY (*glancing about her contentedly*). It's one of the oldest houses in Brooklyn. It's just as it was when Grandfather Brewster built and furnished it—except for the electricity—and we use it as little as possible. It was Mortimer who persuaded us to put it in.

DR. HARPER (*beginning to freeze*). Yes, I can understand that. Your nephew Mortimer seems to live only by electric light.

ABBY. The poor boy has to work so late. I understand he's taking Elaine with him to the theatre again tonight. Teddy, your brother Mortimer will be here a little later.

TEDDY (*baring his teeth in a broad grin*). Dee-lighted!

ABBY (*to* DR. HARPER). We're so happy it's Elaine Mortimer takes to the theatre with him.

DR. HARPER. Well, it's a new experience for me to wait up until three o'clock in the morning for my daughter to be brought home.

ABBY. Oh, Dr. Harper, I hope you don't disapprove of Mortimer.

DR. HARPER. Well——

ABBY. We'd feel so guilty if you did—sister Martha and I. I mean since it was here in our home that your daughter met Mortimer.

DR. HARPER. Of course, Miss Abby. And so I'll say immediately that I believe Mortimer himself to be quite a worthy gentleman. But I must also admit that I have watched the growing intimacy between him and my daughter with some trepidation. For one reason, Miss Abby.

ABBY. You mean his stomach, Dr. Harper?

DR. HARPER. Stomach?

ABBY. His dyspepsia—he's bothered with it so, poor boy.

DR. HARPER. No, Miss Abby, I'll be frank with you. I'm speaking of your nephew's unfortunate connection with the theatre.

ABBY. The theatre! Oh, no, Dr. Harper! Mortimer writes for a New York newspaper.

DR. HARPER. I know, Miss Abby, I know. But a dramatic critic is constantly exposed to the theatre, and I don't doubt but what some of them do develop an interest in it.

ABBY. Well, not Mortimer. You need have no fear of that. Why, Mortimer hates the theatre.

DR. HARPER. Really?

ABBY. Oh, yes! He writes awful things about the theatre. But you can't blame him, poor boy. He was so happy writing about real estate, which he really knew something about, and then they just made him take this terrible night position.

DR. HARPER. My! My!

ABBY. But, as he says, the theatre can't last much longer anyway, and in the meantime it's a living. (*Complacently.*) Yes, I think if we give the theatre another year or two, perhaps... (*There is a knock on R. door.*) Well, now, who do you suppose that is? (*They all rise as* ABBY *goes to door R.* TEDDY *starts for door at the same time but* ABBY *stops him.*) No, thank you, Teddy, I'll go. (*she opens door to admit two policemen,* OFFICERS BROPHY *and* KLEIN.) Come in, Mr. Brophy.

BROPHY. Hello, Miss Brewster.

ABBY. How are you, Mr. Klein?

KLEIN. Very well, Miss Brewster.

(*The two* COPS *cross to* TEDDY *who is standing near desk, and salute him.* TEDDY *returns the salute.*)

TEDDY. What news have you brought me?

BROPHY. Colonel, we have nothing to report.

TEDDY. Splendid! Thank you, gentlemen! At ease!

(*The* COPS *relax and drop* D.S. ABBY *has closed door, and turns to* COPS.)

ABBY. You know Dr. Harper.

KLEIN. Sure! Hello, Dr. Harper.

BROPHY (*turns to* ABBY, *doffing cap*). We've come for the toys for the Christmas Fund.

ABBY. Oh, yes.

DR. HARPER (*standing below table*). That's a splendid work you men do—fixing up discarded toys to give poor children a happier Christmas.

KLEIN. It gives us something to do when we have to sit around the station. You get tired playing cards and then you start cleaning your gun, and the first thing you know you've shot yourself in the foot. (KLEIN *drifts U.L. around to the window-seat.*)

ABBY (*crossing to* TEDDY). Teddy, go upstairs and get that big box from your Aunt Martha's room. (TEDDY *crosses upstage toward stairs.* ABBY *speaks to* BROPHY.) How is Mrs. Brophy to-day? Mrs. Brophy has been quite ill, Dr. Harper.

BROPHY (*to* DR. HARPER). Pneumonia!

DR. HARPER. I'm sorry to hear that.

(TEDDY *has reached the first landing on the stairs where he stops and draws an imaginary sword.*)

TEDDY (*shouting*). CHARGE! (*He charges upstairs and exits off balcony. The others pay no attention to this.*)

BROPHY. Oh, she's better now. A little weak still——

ABBY (*starting towards kitchen*). I'm going to get you some beef broth to take to her.

BROPHY. Don't bother, Miss Abby! You've done so much for her already.

ABBY (*at kitchen door*). We made it this morning. Sister Martha is taking some to poor Mr.Benitzky right now. I won't be a minute. Sit down and be comfortable, all of you. (*She exits into kitchen.*)

(DR. HARPER *sits again.* BROPHY *crosses to table and addresses the other two.*)

BROPHY. She shouldn't go to all that trouble.

KLEIN. Listen, try to stop her or her sister from doing something nice—and for nothing! They don't even care how you vote. (*He sits on window-seat.*)

DR. HARPER. When I received my call to Brooklyn and moved next door my wife wasn't well. When she died and for months before—well, if I know what pure kindness and absolute generosity are, it's because I've known the Brewster sisters.

(*At this moment* TEDDY *steps out on balcony and blows a bugle call. They all look.*)

BROPHY (*stepping* U. S. . . . *Remonstrating*). Colonel, you promised not to do that.

TEDDY. But I have to call a Cabinet meeting to get the release of those supplies. (TEDDY *wheels and exits.*)

BROPHY. He used to do that in the middle of the night. The neighbours raised cain with us. They're a little afraid of him, anyway.

DR. HARPER. Oh, he's quite harmless.

KLEIN. Suppose he does think he's Teddy Roosevelt. There's a lot worse people he could think he was.

BROPHY. Damn shame—a nice family like this hatching a cuckoo.

KLEIN. Well, his father—the old girls' brother, was some sort of a genius, wasn't he? And their father—Teddy's grandfather— seems to me I've heard he was a little crazy too.

BROPHY. Yeah—he was crazy like a fox. He made a million dollars.

DR. HARPER. Really? Here in Brooklyn?

BROPHY. Yeah. Patent medicine. He was a kind of a quack of some sort. Old Sergeant Edwards remembers him. He used the house here as sort of a clinic—tried 'em out on people.

KLEIN. Yeah, I hear he used to make mistakes occasionally, too.

BROPHY. The department never bothered him much because he was pretty useful on autopsies sometimes. Especially poison cases.

KLEIN. Well, whatever he did he left his daughters fixed for life. Thank God for that——

BROPHY. Not that they spend any of it on themselves.

DR. HARPER. Yes, I'm well acquainted with their charities.

KLEIN. You don't know a tenth of it. When I was with the Missing Persons Bureau I was trying to trace an old man that we never did find (*rises*)— do you know there's a renting agency that's got this house down on its list for furnished rooms? They don't rent rooms—but you can bet that anybody who comes here looking for a room goes away with a good meal and probably a few dollars in their kick.

BROPHY. It's just their way of digging up people to do some good to.

(*The* R. *door opens and* MARTHA BREWSTER *enters.* MARTHA *is also a sweet elderly woman with Victorian charm. She is dressed in the old-fashioned manner of* ABBY, *but with a high lace collar that covers her neck.* MEN *all on feet.*)

MARTHA (*at door*). Well, now, isn't this nice? (*Closes door.*)

BROPHY (*crosses to* MARTHA). Good afternoon, Miss Brewster.

MARTHA. How do you do, Mr.Brophy? Dr. Harper. Mr. Klein.

KLEIN. How are you, Miss Brewster? We dropped in to get the Christmas toys.

MARTHA. Oh, yes, Teddy's Army and Navy. They wear out. They're all packed. (*She turns to stairs.* BROPHY *stops her.*)

BROPHY. The Colonel's upstairs after them—it seems the Cabinet has to O.K. it.

MARTHA. Yes, of course. I hope Mrs. Brophy's better?

BROPHY. She's doin' fine, ma'am. Your sister's getting some soup for me to take to her.

MARTHA (*crossing below* BROPHY *to* C.). Oh, yes, we made it this morning. I just took some to a poor man who broke ever so many bones.

(ABBY *enters from kitchen carrying a covered pail.*)

ABBY. Oh, you're back, Martha. How was Mr. Benitzky?

MARTHA. Well, dear, it's pretty serious, I'm afraid. The doctor was there. He's going to amputate in the morning.

ABBY (*hopefully*). Can we be present?

MARTHA (*disappointment*). No. I asked him, but he says it's against the rules of the hospital. (MARTHA *crosses to sideboard, puts pail down. Then puts cape and hat on small table* U. L.)

(TEDDY *enters on balcony with large cardboard box and comes downstairs to desk, putting box on stool.* KLEIN *crosses to toy box.* DR. HARPER *speaks through this.*)

DR. HARPER. You couldn't be of any service—and you must spare yourselves something.

ABBY (*to* BROPHY). Here's the broth, Mr.Brophy. Be sure it's good and hot.

BROPHY. Yes, ma'am (*drops* U. S.)

KLEIN. This is fine—it'll make a lot of kids happy (*lifts out toy soldier*). That O'Malley boy is nuts about soldiers.

TEDDY. That's General Miles. I've retired him. (KLEIN *removes ship.*) What's this! The Oregon!

MARTHA (*crosses to* U. L.). Teddy, dear, put it back.

TEDDY. But the Oregon goes to Australia.

ABBY. Now, Teddy——

TEDDY. No, I've given my word to Fighting Bob Evans.

MARTHA. But, Teddy——

KLEIN. What's the difference what kid gets it—Bobby Evans, Izzy Cohen? (*Crosses to* R. *door with box, opens door.* BROPHY *follows.*) We'll run along, ma'am, and thank you very much.

ABBY. Not at all. (*The two* COPS *stop in doorway, salute* TEDDY *and exit.* ABBY *crosses and shuts door as she speaks.* TEDDY *starts upstairs.*) Goodbye.

DR. HARPER (*crosses to sofa, gets hat*). I must be getting home.

ABBY. Before you go, Dr. Harper——

(TEDDY *has reached stair landing.*)

TEDDY. CHARGE! (*He dashes up the stairs. At the top he stops and with a sweeping gesture over the balcony rail, invites all to follow him as he speaks.*) Charge the blockhouse! (*He dashes through door, closing it after him.*)

(DR. HARPER *looks after him.* MARTHA, *to* L. *of* DR. HARPER, *is fooling with a brooch on her dress.* ABBY R. *of* DR. HARPER.)

DR. HARPER. The blockhouse?

MARTHA. The stairs are always San Juan Hill.

DR. HARPER. Have you ever tried to persuade him that he wasn't Teddy Roosevelt?

ABBY. Oh, no!

MARTHA. He's so happy being Teddy Roosevelt.

ABBY. Once, a long time ago—(*She crosses below to* MARTHA) remember, Martha? We thought if he would be George Washington it might be a change for him——

MARTHA. But he stayed under his bed for days and just wouldn't be anybody.

ABBY. And we'd so much rather he'd be Mr.Roosevelt than nobody.

DR. HARPER. Well, if he's happy—and what's more important you're happy—(*he takes blue-backed legal paper from inside pocket*) you'll see that he signs these.

MARTHA. What are they?

ABBY. Dr. Harper has made all arrangements for Teddy to go to Happy Dale Sanatorium after we pass on.

MARTHA. But why should Teddy sign any papers now?

DR. HARPER. It's better to have it all settled. If the Lord should take you away suddenly perhaps we couldn't persuade Teddy to commit himself and that would mean an unpleasant legal procedure. Mr. Witherspoon understands they're to be filed away until the time comes to use them.

MARTHA. Mr.Witherspoon? Who's he?

DR. HARPER. He's the Superintendent of Happy Dale.

ABBY (*to Martha*). Dr. Harper has arranged for him to drop in tomorrow or the next day to meet Teddy.

DR. HARPER (*crossing to* R. *door and opening it*). I'd better be running along or Elaine will be over here looking for me.

(ABBY *crosses to door and calls after him.*)

ABBY. Give our love to Elaine—and Dr. Harper, please don't think harshly of Mortimer because he's a dramatic critic.

Somebody has to do those things. (ABBY *closes door, comes back into room.*)

(MARTHA *crosses to sideboard, puts legal papers on it. . . notices tea things on table.*)

MARTHA. Did you just have tea? Isn't it rather late?

ABBY (*as one who has a secret*). Yes—and dinner's going to be late too.

(TEDDY *enters on balcony, starts downstairs to first landing.* MARTHA *steps to* ABBY.)

MARTHA. So? Why?

ABBY. Teddy! (TEDDY *stops on landing.*) Good news for you. You're going to Panama and dig another lock for the canal.

TEDDY. Dee-lighted! That's bully! Just bully! I shall prepare at once for the journey. (*He turns to go upstairs, stops as if puzzled, hurries back to landing, cries* CHARGE! *and rushes up and off.*)

MARTHA (*elated*). Abby! While I was out?

ABBY (*taking* MARTHA'S *hands*). Yes, dear! I just couldn't wait for you. I didn't know when you'd be back and Dr. Harper was coming.

MARTHA. But all by yourself?

ABBY. Oh, I got along fine!

MARTHA. I'll run right downstairs and see. (*She starts happily for cellar door.*)

ABBY. Oh, no, there wasn't time, and I was all alone.

(MARTHA *looks around the room towards kitchen.*)

MARTHA. Well——

ABBY (*coyly*). Martha—just look in the window-seat. (MARTHA *almost skips to window-seat, and just as she gets there a knock is heard on the* R. *door. She stops. They both look toward door.* ABBY *hurries to door and opens it.* ELAINE HARPER *enters.* ELAINE *is an attractive girl in her twenties; she looks surprisingly smart for a minister's daughter.*) Oh, it's Elaine. (*Opens door.*) Come in, dear.

(ELAINE *crosses to* C. ABBY *closes door, crosses to* C.)

ELAINE. Good afternoon, Miss Abby. Good afternoon, Miss Martha. I thought Father was here.

MARTHA (*stepping to* L. *of table*). He just this minute left. Didn't you meet him?

ELAINE (*pointing to window in* L. *wall*). No, I took the short cut through the cemetery. Mortimer hasn't come yet?

ABBY. No, dear.

ELAINE. Oh? He asked me to meet him here. Do you mind if I wait?

MARTHA. Not at all.

ABBY. Why don't you sit down, dear?

MARTHA. But we really must speak to Mortimer about doing this to you.

ELAINE (*sits chair* R. *of table*). Doing what?

MARTHA. Well, he was brought up to know better. When a gentleman is taking a young lady out he should call for her at her house.

ELAINE (*to both*). Oh, there's something about calling for a girl at a parsonage that discourages any man who doesn't embroider.

ABBY. He's done this too often—we're going to speak to him.

ELAINE. Oh, please don't. After young men whose idea of night life was to take me to prayer meeting, it's wonderful to go to the theatre almost every night of my life.

MARTHA. It's comforting for us too, because if Mortimer has to see some of those plays he has to see—at least he's sitting next to a minister's daughter. (MARTHA *steps to back of table*.)

(ABBY *crosses to back of table, starts putting tea things on tray.* ELAINE *and* MARTHA *help*.)

ABBY. My goodness, Elaine, what must you think of us—not having tea cleared away by this time. (*She picks up tray and exits to kitchen*.)

(MARTHA *blows out one candle and takes it to sideboard.* ELAINE *blows out other, takes to sideboard*.)

MARTHA (*as* ABBY *exits*). Now don't bother with anything in the kitchen until Mortimer comes, and then I'll help you. (*To* ELAINE.) Mortimer should be here any minute now.

ELAINE. Yes. Father must have been surprised not to find me at home. I'd better run over and say goodnight to him. (*She crosses to* R. *door.*)

MARTHA. It's a shame you missed him, dear.

ELAINE (*opening door*). If Mortimer comes you tell him I'll be right back. (*She has opened door, but sees* MORTIMER *just outside.*) Hello, Mort!

(MORTIMER BREWSTER *walks in. He is a dramatic critic.*)

MORTIMER. Hello, Elaine. (*As he passes her going toward* MARTHA, *thus placing himself between* ELAINE *and* MARTHA, *he reaches back and pats* ELAINE *on the fanny . . . then embraces* MARTHA.) Hello, Aunt Martha.

(MARTHA *exits to kitchen, calling as she goes.*)

MARTHA. Abby, Mortimer's here!

(ELAINE *slowly closes door.*)

MORTIMER (*turning* R.). Were you going somewhere?

ELAINE. I was just going over to tell Father not to wait up for me.

MORTIMER. I didn't know that was still being done, even in Brooklyn. (*He throws his hat on sofa.*)

(ABBY *enters from kitchen.* MARTHA *follows, stays in doorway,* R.)

ABBY (*crosses to* MORTIMER *at* C.). Hello, Mortimer.

MORTIMER (*embraces her and kisses her*). Hello, Aunt Abby.

ABBY. How are you, dear?

MORTIMER. All right. And you look well. You haven't changed much since yesterday.

ABBY. Oh, my goodness, it was yesterday wasn't it? We're seeing a great deal of you lately. (*She crosses and starts to sit in chair above table.*) Well, come, sit down. Sit down.

(MARTHA *stops her from sitting.*)

MARTHA. Abby—haven't we something to do in the kitchen?

ABBY. Huh?

MARTHA. You know—the tea things.

ABBY (*suddenly seeing* MORTIMER *and* ELAINE, *and catching on*). Oh, yes! Yes! The tea things——(*She backs towards the kitchen.*)Well—you two just make yourselves at home. Just——

MARTHA. —make yourselves at home.

(*They exit kitchen door,* ABBY *closing door.*)

ELAINE (*stepping to* MORTIMER, *ready to be kissed*). Well, can't you take a hint?

MORTIMER (*complaining*). No. . .that was pretty obvious. A lack of inventiveness, I should say.

ELAINE (*only slightly annoyed as she crosses to table, and puts handbag on it*). Yes—that's exactly what you'd say.

MORTIMER (*He is at desk, fishing various pieces of notepaper from his pockets, and separating dollar bills that are mixed in with papers.*) Where do you want to go for dinner?

ELAINE (*opening bag, looking in hand mirror*). I don't care. I'm not very hungry.

MORTIMER. Well, I just had breakfast. Suppose we wait until after the show?

ELAINE. But that'll make it pretty late, won't it?

MORTIMER. Not with the little stinker we're seeing tonight. From what I've heard about it we'll be at Blake's by ten o'clock.

ELAINE (*crosses to* U. S. C.). You ought to be fair to these plays.

MORTIMER. Are these plays fair to me?

ELAINE. *I've* never seen you walk out on a musical.

MORTIMER. That musical isn't opening tonight.

ELAINE (*disappointed*). No?

MORTIMER. Darling, you'll have to learn the rules. With a musical there are always four changes of title and three postponements. They liked it in New Haven but it needs a lot of work.

ELAINE. Oh, I was hoping it was a musical.

MORTIMER. You have such a light mind.

ELAINE. Not a bit. Musicals somehow have a humanising effect on you. (*He gives her a look.*) After a serious play we join the proletariat in the subway and I listen to a lecture on the drama. After a musical you bring me home in a taxi (*turning away*), and you make a few passes.

MORTIMER (*crossing D. C.*). Now wait a minute, darling, that's a very inaccurate piece of reporting.

ELAINE (*leaning against D. S. end of table*). Oh, I will admit that after the Behrman play you told me I had authentic beauty—and that's a hell of a thing to say to a girl. It wasn't until after our first musical you told me I had nice legs. And I have too.

(MORTIMER *stares at her legs for a moment, then walks over and kisses her.*)

MORTIMER. For a minister's daughter you know a lot about life. Where'd you learn it?

ELAINE (*casually*). In the choir loft.

MORTIMER. I'll explain that to you some time, darling—the close connection between eroticism and religion.

ELAINE. Religion never gets as high as the choir loft. (*Crosses below table, gathers up bag.*) Which reminds me, I'd better tell Father please not to wait up for me tonight.

MORTIMER (*almost to himself*). I've never been able to rationalise it.

ELAINE. What?

MORTIMER. My falling in love with a girl who lives in Brooklyn.

ELAINE. Falling in love? You're not stooping to the articulate, are you,

MORTIMER (*ignoring this*). The only way I can regain my self respect is to keep you in New York.

ELAINE (*few steps toward him*). Did you say keep?

MORTIMER. No, no. I've come to the conclusion that you're holding out for the legalities.

ELAINE (*crossing to him as he backs away*). I can afford to be a good girl for quite a few years yet.

MORTIMER (*stops and embraces her*). And I can't wait that long. Where could we be married in a hurry—say tonight?

ELAINE. I'm afraid Father will insist on officiating.

MORTIMER (*turning away* R. *from her*). Oh God! I'll bet your father could make even the marriage service sound pedestrian.

ELAINE. Are you by any chance writing a review of it?

MORTIMER. Forgive me, darling. It's an occupational disease. (*She smiles at him lovingly and walks toward him. He meets her halfway and they forget themselves for a moment in a sentimental embrace and kiss. When they come out of it, he turns away from her quickly . . . breaking* U. S. *near desk.*) I may give that play tonight a good notice.

ELAINE. Now, darling, don't pretend you love me that much.

MORTIMER (*looks at her with polite lechery, then starts toward her*). Be sure to tell your father not to wait up tonight.

ELAINE (*aware that she can't trust either of them, and backing* U. S.). I think tonight I'd better tell him to wait up.

MORTIMER (*following her*). I'll telephone Winchell to publish the banns.

ELAINE (*backing* D. S.). Nevertheless——

MORTIMER. All right, everything formal and legal. But not later than next month.

ELAINE (*runs into his arms*). Darling! I'll talk it over with Father and set the date.

MORTIMER. No—we'll have to see what's in rehearsal. There'll be a lot of other first nights in October.

(TEDDY *enters from balcony and comes down the stairs dressed in tropical clothes and a solar topee. At foot of stairs he sees* MORTIMER, *crosses to him and shakes hands.*)

TEDDY. Hello, Mortimer!

MORTIMER (*gravely*). How are you, Mr. President?

TEDDY. Bully, thank you. Just bully! What news have you brought me?

MORTIMER. Just this, Mr. President—the country is squarely behind you.

TEDDY (*beaming*). Yes, I know. Isn't it wonderful? (*He shakes* MORTIMER'S *hand again.*) Well, goodbye. (*He crosses to* ELAINE *and shakes hands with her.*) Goodbye. (*He goes to cellar door.*)

ELAINE. Where are you off to, Teddy?

TEDDY. Panama. (*He exits through cellar door, shutting it.* ELAINE *looks at* MORTIMER *inquiringly.*)

MORTIMER. Panama's the cellar. He digs locks for the canal down there.

(ELAINE *takes his arm and they stroll* D. L. *to* R. *of table.*)

ELAINE. You're so sweet with him—and he's very fond of you.

MORTIMER. Well, Teddy was always my favourite brother.

ELAINE (*stopping and turning to him*). Favourite? Were there more of you?

MORTIMER. There's another brother—Jonathan.

ELAINE. I never heard of him. Your aunts never mention him.

MORTIMER. No, we don't like to talk about Jonathan. He left Brooklyn very early—by request. Jonathan was the kind of boy who liked to cut worms in two—with his teeth.

ELAINE. What became of him?

MORTIMER. I don't know. He wanted to become a surgeon like Grandfather but he wouldn't go to medical school first and his practice got him into trouble.

(ABBY *enters from kitchen, crossing* D. L. *of table.*)

ABBY. Aren't you two going to be late for the theatre?

(MORTIMER'S *left arm around* ELAINE'S *neck, he looks at his wrist-watch.*)

MORTIMER. We're skipping dinner. We won't have to start for half an hour.

ABBY (*backing* U. L.). Well, then I'll leave you two alone together again.

ELAINE. Don't bother, darling. (*Breaking* R. *in front of* MORTIMER.) I'm going to run over to speak to Father. (*To* MORTIMER.)

Before I go out with you he likes to pray over me a little. (*She runs to* R. *door and opens it, keeping her left hand on outside door-knob.*) I'll be right back—I'll cut through the cemetery.

MORTIMER (*crosses to her, puts his hand on hers*). If the prayer isn't too long, I'd have time to lead you beside distilled waters.

(ELAINE *laughs and exits.* MORTIMER *shuts door.*)

ABBY (*happily, as she crosses to* C.). Mortimer, that's the first time I've ever heard you quote the Bible. We knew Elaine would be a good influence for you.

MORTIMER (*laughs, crosses* L., *then turns to* ABBY). Oh, by the way—I'm going to marry her.

ABBY. What? Oh, darling! (*She runs to him and embraces him. Then she dashes toward kitchen door as* MORTIMER *crosses to window* L. *and looks out.*) Martha, Martha! (MARTHA *enters from kitchen.*) Come right in here. I've got the most wonderful news for you— Mortimer and Elaine are going to be married.

MARTHA. Married? Oh, Mortimer! (*She runs over to* R. *of* MORTIMER, *who is looking out window* L., *embraces and kisses him.* ABBY *comes down to his* L. *He has his arms around both of them.*)

ABBY. We hoped it would happen just like this.

MARTHA. Well, Elaine must be the happiest girl in the world.

MORTIMER (*pulls curtain back, looks out window*). Happy! Just look at her leaping over those gravestones. (*As he looks out window* MORTIMER'S *attention is suddenly drawn to something.*) Say! What's that?

MARTHA (*looking out on his* R. ABBY *is on his* L.). What's what, dear?

MORTIMER. See that statue there. That's a horundinida carnina.

MARTHA. Oh, no, dear—that's Emma B. Stout ascending to heaven.

MORTIMER. No, no,—standing on Mrs. Stout's left ear. That bird—that's a red-crested swallow. I've only seen one of those before in my life.

ABBY (*crossing around above table and pushes chair* R. *into table*). I don't know how you can be thinking about a bird now—what with Elaine and the engagement and everything.

MORTIMER. It's a vanishing species. (*He turns away from window.*) Thoreau was very fond of them. (*As he crosses to desk to look through various drawers and papers.*) By the way, I left a large envelope around here last week. It was one of the chapters of my book on Thoreau. Have you seen it?

MARTHA (*pushing armchair into table*). Well, if you left it here it must be here somewhere.

ABBY (*crossing to* D. L. *of* MORTIMER). When are you going to be married? What are your plans? There must be something more you can tell us about Elaine.

MORTIMER. Elaine? Oh, yes, Elaine thought it was brilliant. (*He crosses to sideboard, looks through cupboards and drawers.*)

MARTHA. What was, dear?

MORTIMER. My chapter on Thoreau. (*He finds a bundle of papers (script) in* R. *drawer and takes them to table and looks through them.*)

ABBY (*at* C.). Well, when Elaine comes back I think we ought to have a little celebration. We must drink to your happiness. Martha, isn't there some of that Lady Baltimore cake left?

(*During the last few speeches* MARTHA *has picked up pail from sideboard and her cape and hat and gloves from table in* U. L. *corner.*)

MARTHA (*crossing* D. L.). Oh, yes!

ABBY. And I'll open a bottle of wine.

MARTHA (*as she exits to kitchen*). Oh, and to think it happened in this room!

MORTIMER (*has finished looking through papers, is gazing around room*). Now where could I have put that?

ABBY. Well, with your fiancée sitting beside you tonight, I do hope the play will be something you can enjoy for once. It may be something romantic. What's the name of it?

MORTIMER. ''Murder Will Out''.

ABBY. Oh dear! (*She disappears into the kitchen as* MORTIMER *goes on talking.*)

MORTIMER. When the curtain goes up the first thing you'll see will be a dead body. (*He lifts window-seat and sees one. Not believing it, he drops the window-seat again and starts downstage. He suddenly stops with a "take," then goes back, throws window-seat open and stares in. He goes slightly mad for a moment. He backs away and then hears* ABBY *humming on her way into the room. He drops the window-seat again and holds it (a pad that goes under tablecloth) down, staring around the room.* ABBY *enters carrying a silencer and tablecloth which she puts on the armchair, then picks up bundle of papers and returns them to drawer in sideboard.* MORTIMER *speaks to her in a somewhat strained voice.*) Aunt Abby!

ABBY (*at sideboard*). Yes, dear?

MORTIMER. You were going to make plans for Teddy to go to that . . . sanatorium—Happy Dale——

ABBY (*bringing legal papers from sideboard to* MORTIMER). Yes, dear, it's all arranged. Dr. Harper was here today and brought the papers for Teddy to sign. Here they are.

(*He takes them from her.*)

MORTIMER. He's got to sign them right away.

ABBY (*arranging silencer on table.* MARTHA *enters from kitchen door with table silver and plates on a tray. She sets tray on sideboard. Goes to table* R.). That's what Dr. Harper thinks. Then there won't be any legal difficulties after we pass on.

MORTIMER. He's got to sign them this minute! He's down in the cellar—get him up here right away.

MARTHA (*unfolding tablecloth. She's above table on* R.). There's no such hurry as that.

ABBY. No. When Teddy starts working on the canal you can't get his mind on anything else.

MORTIMER. Teddy's got to go to Happy Dale now—tonight.

MARTHA. Oh, no, dear, that's not until after we're gone.

MORTIMER. Right away, I tell you!—right away!

ABBY (*turning to* MORTIMER). Why, Mortimer, how can you say such a thing? Why as long as we live we'll never be separated from Teddy.

MORTIMER. (*trying to be calm*). Listen, darlings, I'm frightfully sorry, but I've got some shocking news for you. (*The* AUNTS *stop work and look at him with some interest.*) Now we've all got to try and keep our heads. You know we've sort of humoured Teddy because we thought he was harmless!

MARTHA. Why he *is* harmless!

MORTIMER. He *was* harmless. That's why he has to go to Happy Dale. Why he has to be confined.

ABBY (*stepping to* MORTIMER). Mortimer, why have you suddenly turned against Teddy?—your own brother?

MORTIMER. You've got to know sometime. It might as well be now. Teddy's—killed a man!

MARTHA. Nonsense, dear.

(MORTIMER *rises and points to window-seat.*)

MORTIMER. There's a body in the window-seat!

ABBY. Yes, dear, we know.

(MORTIMER *"takes" as* ABBY *and* MARTHA *busy themselves again at table.*)

MARTHA. You *know*?

MARTHA. Of course, dear, but it has nothing to do with Teddy. (*Gets tray from sideboard—arranges silver and plates on table: three places,* U. L. *and* R.*).*

ABBY. Now, Mortimer, just forget about it—forget you ever saw the gentleman.

MORTIMER. *Forget*?

ABBY. We never dreamed you'd peek.

MORTIMER. But who is he?

ABBY. His name's Hoskins—Adam Hoskins. That's really all I know about him—except that he's a Methodist.

MORTIMER. That's all you know about him? Well, what's he doing here? What happened to him?

MARTHA. He died.

MORTIMER. Aunt Martha, men don't just get into window-seats and die.

ABBY (*silly boy*). No, he died first.

MORTIMER. Well, how?

ABBY. Oh, Mortimer, don't be so inquisitive. The gentleman died because he drank some wine with poison in it.

MORTIMER. How did the poison get in the wine?

MARTHA. Well, we put it in wine because it's less noticeable—when it's in tea it has a distinct odour.

MORTIMER. *You* put it in the wine?

ABBY. Yes. And I put Mr. Hoskins in the window-seat because Dr. Harper was coming.

MORTIMER. So you knew what you'd done! You didn't want Dr. Harper to see the body!

ABBY. Well, not at tea—that wouldn't have been very nice. Now, Mortimer, you know the whole thing, just forget about it. I do think Martha and I have the right to our own little secrets. (*She crosses to sideboard to get two goblets from* L. *cupboard as* MARTHA *comes to table from sideboard with salt dish and pepper shaker.*)

MARTHA. And don't you tell Elaine! (*She gets third goblet from sideboard, then turns to* ABBY *who takes tray from sideboard.*) Oh, Abby, while I was out I dropped in on Mrs. Schultz. She's much better but she would like us to take Junior to the movies again.

ABBY. Well, we must do that tomorrow or next day.

MARTHA. Yes, but this time we'll go where we want to go. (*She starts for kitchen door.* ABBY *follows.*) Junior's not going to drag me into another one of those scary pictures. (*They exit into kitchen as* MORTIMER *wheels around and looks after them.* ABBY *shuts door.*)

MORTIMER (*dazed, looks around the room. His eyes come to rest on telephone on desk; he crosses to it and dials a number. Into phone.*) City desk! (*There is a pause.*) Hello, Al. Do you know who this is? (*Pause.*) That's right. Say, Al, when I left the office, I told you where I was going, remember?—Well, where did I say? (*Pause.*) Uh-huh. Well, it would take me about half an hour to get to Brooklyn. What time have you got? (*He looks at his watch.*) That's right. I must be here. (*He hangs up, sits for a minute, then suddenly leaps off stool toward kitchen.*) Aunt Abby! Aunt Martha! Come in here! (*He backs to* C. *stage as the two* AUNTS *bustle in.* MARTHA *has tray with plates, cups, saucers and soup cups.*) What are we going to do? What are we going to do?

MARTHA (R. *of table*). What are we going to do about what, dear?

MORTIMER (*pointing to window-seat*). There's a body in there.

ABBY (U. L. *of* MORTIMER). Yes—Mr. Hoskins.

MORTIMER. Well, good heavens, I can't turn you over to the police! But what am I going to do?

MARTHA. Well, for one thing, dear, stop being so excited.

ABBY. And for pity's sake stop worrying. We told you to forget the whole thing.

MORTIMER. Forget! My dear Aunt Abby, can't I make you realise that something has to be done?

ABBY (*a little sharply*). Now, Mortimer, you behave yourself. You're too old to be flying off the handle like this.

MORTIMER. But Mr. Hotchkiss——

(ABBY, *on her way to sideboard, stops and turns to* MORTIMER.)

ABBY. Hoskins, dear. (*She continues on her way to sideboard and gets napkins and rings from L. drawer.* MARTHA *puts her tray, with cups, plates, etc., on table.* MORTIMER *continues speaking through this.*)

MORTIMER. Well, whatever his name is, you can't leave him there.

MARTHA. We don't intend to, dear.

ABBY (*crossing to table L. with napkins and rings*). No, Teddy's down in the cellar now digging the lock.

MORTIMER. You mean you're going to bury Mr. Hotchkiss in the cellar?

MARTHA (*stepping to him*). Oh, yes, dear,—that's what we did with the others.

MORTIMER (*walking away to R.*). No! You can't bury Mr. —(*Double take. Turns back to them.*)—others?

ABBY. The other gentlemen.

MORTIMER. When you say others—do you mean—other? More than one others?

MARTHA. Oh, yes, dear. Let me see, this is eleven. (*To* ABBY U. L. *of table.*) Isn't it, Abby?

ABBY. No, dear, this makes twelve.

(MORTIMER *backs away from them stunned, toward phone stool at desk.*)

MARTHA. Oh, I think you're wrong, Abby. This is only eleven.

ABBY. No dear, because I remember when Mr. Hoskins first came in, it occured to me that he would make just an even dozen.

MARTHA. Well, you really shouldn't count the first one.

ABBY. Oh, I was counting the first one. So that makes it twelve.

(*The phone rings.* MORTIMER *in a daze, turns toward it and without picking up receiver, speaks.*)

MORTIMER. Hello! (*He comes to, and picks up receiver.*) Hello. Oh, hello, Al. My, it's good to hear your voice.

(ABBY, *at table, is still holding out for a "twelve" count.*)

ABBY. Well, anyway, they're all down in the cellar——

MORTIMER (*to* AUNTS). Sshhhh—— (*Into phone, as* AUNTS *cross to sideboard and put candelabras from top shelf to bottom shelf.*) Oh, no, Al, I'm sober as a lark. I just called you because I was feeling a little Pirandello—Piran—you wouldn't know, Al. Look, I'm glad you called. Get hold of George right away. He's got to review the play tonight. I can't make it. No, Al, you're wrong. I'll tell you it tomorrow. Well, George has got to cover the play tonight! This is my department and I'm running it! You get ahold of George! (*He hangs up and sits for a moment trying to collect himself.*) Now let's see, where were we? (*He suddenly leaps from stool.*) TWELVE!

MARTHA. Yes, Abby thinks we ought to count the first one and that makes twelve. (*She goes back to sideboard.*)

(MORTIMER *takes chair* R. *of table and faces it toward* R. *stage, then takes* MARTHA *by the hand, leads her to chair and sets her in it.*)

MORTIMER. All right—now—who was the first one?

ABBY (*crossing from above table to* MORTIMER). Mr. Midgely. He was a Baptist.

MARTHA. Of course, I still think we can't claim full credit for him because he just died.

ABBY. Martha means without any help from us. You see, Mr. Midgely came here looking for a room——

MARTHA. It was right after you moved to New York.

ABBY. — And it didn't seem right for that lovely room to be going to waste when there were so many people who needed it——

MARTHA. — He was such a lonely old man . . .

ABBY. All his kith and kin were dead and it left him so forlorn and unhappy ——

MARTHA. — We felt so sorry for him.

ABBY. And then when his heart attack came—and he sat dead in that chair (*pointing to armchair*) looking so peaceful—remember, Martha—we made up our minds then and there that if we could help other lonely old men to that same peace—we would!

MORTIMER (*all ears*). He dropped dead right in that chair! How awful for you!

MARTHA. Oh, no, dear. Why, it was rather like old times. Your grandfather always used to have a cadaver or two around the house. You see, Teddy had been digging in Panama and he thought Mr. Midgely was a Yellow Fever victim.

ABBY. That meant he had to be buried immediately.

MARTHA. So we all took him down to Panama and put him in the lock. (*She rises, puts her arm around* ABBY.) Now that's why we told you not to worry about it because we know exactly what's to be done.

MORTIMER. And that's how all this started—that man walking in here and dropping dead.

ABBY. Of course, we realised we couldn't depend on that happening again. So——

MARTHA (*crosses to* MORTIMER). You remember those jars of poison that have been up on the shelves in Grandfather's laboratory all these years——?

ABBY. You know your Aunt Martha's knack for mixing things. You've eaten enough of her piccalilli.

MARTHA. Well, dear, for a gallon of elderberry wine I take one teaspoonful of arsenic, then add a half-teaspoonful of strychnine and then just a pinch of cyanide.

MORTIMER (*appraisingly*). Should have quite a kick.

ABBY. Yes! As a matter of fact one of our gentlemen found time to say "How delicious!"

MARTHA (*stepping* U. S.). Well, I'll have to get things started in the kitchen.

ABBY (*to* MORTIMER). I wish you could stay for dinner.

MARTHA. I'm trying out a new recipe.

MORTIMER. I couldn't eat a thing.

(MARTHA *goes out to kitchen.*)

ABBY (*calling after* MARTHA). I'll come and help you, dear. (*She pushes chair* R. *into table.*) Well, I feel so much better now. Oh, you have to wait for Elaine, don't you? (*She smiles.*) How happy you must be. (*She goes to kitchen doorway.*) Well, dear, I'll leave you alone with your thoughts. (*She exits, shutting door.*)

(*The shutting of the door wakes* MORTIMER *from his trance. He crosses to window-seat, kneels down, raises cover, looks in. Not believing, he lowers cover, rubs his eyes, raises cover again. This time he really sees Mr. Hoskins. Closes window-seat hastily, rises, steps back. Runs over and closes curtains over window. Backs up to above table. Sees water glass on table, picks it up, raises it to lips, suddenly remembers that poisoned wine comes in glasses, puts it down quickly. Crosses to cellar door, opens it.* ELAINE *enters* R., *and he closes cellar door with a bang. As* ELAINE *puts her bag on top of desk he looks at her, and it dawns on him that he knows her. He speaks with faint surprise.*)

MORTIMER. Oh, it's you. (*He drops* D. S. ELAINE *crosses to him, takes his hand.*)

ELAINE. Don't be cross, darling! Father could see that I was excited—so I told him about us and that made it hard for me to get away. But listen, darling—he's not going to wait up for me tonight.

MORTIMER (*looking at window-seat*). You run along home, Elaine, and I'll call you up tomorrow.

ELAINE. Tomorrow!

MORTIMER (*irritated*). You know I always call you up every day or two.

ELAINE. But we're going to the theatre tonight.

MORTIMER. No—no we're not!

ELAINE. Well, why not?

MORTIMER (*turning to her*). Elaine, something's come up.

ELAINE. What, darling? Mortimer—you've lost your job!

MORTIMER. No—no—I haven't lost my job. I'm just not covering that play tonight. (*Pushing her* R.). Now you run along home, Elaine.

ELAINE. But I've got to know what's happened. Certainly you can tell me.

MORTIMER. No, dear, I can't.

ELAINE. But if we're going to be married——

MORTIMER. Married?

ELAINE. Have you forgotten that not fifteen minutes ago you proposed to me?

MORTIMER (*vaguely*). I did? Oh—yes? Well, as far as I know that's still on. (*Urging her* R. *again.*) Now you run along home, Elaine. I've got to do something.

ELAINE. Listen, you can't propose to me one minute and throw me out of the house the next.

MORTIMER (*pleading*). I'm not throwing you out of the house, darling. Will you get out of here?

ELAINE. No. I won't get out of here. (MORTIMER *crosses toward kitchen.* ELAINE *crosses below to window-seat.*) Not until I've had some kind of explanation. (ELAINE *is about to sit on window-seat.* MORTIMER *grabs her by the hand. The phone rings.*)

MORTIMER. Elaine! (*He goes to phone, dragging* ELAINE *with him.*) Oh, hello, Al. Hold on a minute, will you?—All right, it's important! But it can wait a minute, can't it? Hold on! (*He puts receiver on desk. Takes* ELAINE's *bag from top of desk and hands it to her. Then takes her by hand and leads her to door* R. *and opens it.*) Look, Elaine, you're a sweet girl and I love you. But I have something on my mind now and I want you to go home and wait until I call you.

ELAINE (*in doorway*). Don't try to be masterful.

MORTIMER (*annoyed to the point of being literate*). When we're married and I have problems to face I hope you're less tedious and uninspired!

ELAINE. And when we're married, *if* we're married—I hope I find you adequate! (*She exits.* MORTIMER *does take, then runs out on porch after her, calling* —)

MORTIMER. Elaine! Elaine! (*He runs back in, shutting door, crosses and kneels on window-seat to open window. Suddenly remembers contents of window-seat and leaps off it. Dashes into kitchen but remembers Al is on phone, re-enters immediately and crosses to phone.*) Hello, Al? Hello . . . hello . . . (*He pushes hook down and starts to dial when door-bell rings. He thinks it's the phone.* ABBY *enters from kitchen.*) Hello. Hello, Al?

ABBY (*crossing to* R. *door and opening it*). That's the door-bell, dear, not the telephone. (MORTIMER *pushes hook down . . . dials.* MR. GIBBS *steps in doorway* R.). How do you do? Come in.

GIBBS. I understand you have a room to rent.

(MARTHA *enters from kitchen. Puts "Lazy Susan" (Cruet) on sideboard, then gets to* R. *of table.*)

ABBY. Yes. Won't you step in?

GIBBS (*stepping into room*). Are you the lady of the house?

ABBY. Yes, I'm Miss Brewster. And this is my sister, another Miss Brewster.

GIBBS. My name is Gibbs.

ABBY (*easing him to chair* R. *of table*). Oh, won't you sit down? I'm sorry we were just setting the table for dinner.

MORTIMER (*into phone*). Hello—let me talk to Al again. City desk. (*Loud.*) AL!! CITY DESK! WHAT? I'm sorry, wrong number. (*He hangs up and starts dialling again as* GIBBS *looks at him.* GIBBS *turns to* ABBY.)

GIBBS. May I see the room?

MARTHA (D. L. *of table*). Why don't you sit down a minute and let's get acquainted.

GIBBS. That won't do much good if I don't like the room.

ABBY. Is Brooklyn your home?

GIBBS. Haven't got a home. Live in a hotel. Don't like it.

MORTIMER (*into phone*). Hello. City desk.

MARTHA. Are your family Brooklyn people?

GIBBS. Haven't got any family.

ABBY (*Another victim*). ALL alone in the world?

GIBBS. Yep.

ABBY. Well, Martha—— (MARTHA *goes happily to sideboard, gets bottle of wine from* U. L. *cupboard, and a wine glass, and sets them on table,* U. S. *end.* ABBY *eases* GIBBS *into chair* R. *of table and continues speaking to him, then to above table.*) Well, you've come to just the right house. Do sit down.

MORTIMER (*into phone*). Hello, Al? Mort. We got cut off. Al, I can't cover the play tonight—that's all there is to it, I can't!

MARTHA (L. *of table*). What church do you go to? These's an Episcopal church practically next door. (*Her gesture toward window brings her to window-seat and she sits.*)

GIBBS. I'm Presbyterian. Used to be.

MORTIMER (*into phone*). What's George doing in Bermuda? (*Rises and gets loud.*) Certainly I told him he could go to Bermuda—it's my department, isn't it? Well, you've got to get somebody. Who else is there around the office? (*He sits on second chair.*)

GIBBS (*annoyed. Rises and crosses below table to* L. *of it*). Is there always this much noise?

MARTHA. Oh, he doesn't live with us.

(ABBY *sits above table.*)

MORTIMER (*into phone*). There must be somebody around the place. Look, Al, how about the office boy? You know the bright one—the one we don't like? Well, you look around the office, I'll hold on.

GIBBS. I'd really like to see the room.

ABBY (*after seating* GIBBS R. *of table she has sat in chair above table*). It's upstairs. Won't you try a glass of our wine before we start up?

GIBBS. Never touch it.

MARTHA. We make this ourselves. It's elderberry wine.

GIBBS (*to* MARTHA). Elderberry wine. Humph. Haven't tasted elderberry wine since I was a boy. Thank you. (*He pulls armchair around and sits as* ABBY *uncorks bottle and starts to pour wine.*)

MORTIMER (*into phone*). Well, there must be some printers around. Look, Al, the fellow who sets my copy. He ought to know about what I'd write. His name is Joe. He's the third machine from the left. But, Al, he might turn out to be another Burns Mantle!

GIBBS (*to* MARTHA). Do you have your own elderberry bushes?

MARTHA. No, but the cemetery is full of them.

MORTIMER (*rising*). No, I'm not drinking, but I'm going to start now.

GIBBS. Do you serve meals?

ABBY. We might, but first just see whether you like our wine.

(MORTIMER *hangs up, puts phone on top of desk and crosses* L. *He sees wine on table. Goes to sideboard, gets glass, brings it to table and pours a drink.* GIBBS *has his glass in hand and is getting ready to drink.*)

MARTHA (*sees* MORTIMER *pouring wine*). Mortimer! Eh eh eh eh! (GIBBS *stops and looks at* MARTHA. MORTIMER *pays no attention.*) Eh eh eh eh!

(*As* MORTIMER *raises glass to lips with* L. *hand.* ABBY *reaches up and pulls his arm down.*)

ABBY. Mortimer. Not that. (MORTIMER, *still dumb, puts his glass down on table. Then he suddenly sees* GIBBS *who has just got glass to his lips and is about to drink. He points across table at* GIBBS *and gives a wild cry.* GIBBS *looks at him, putting his glass down.* MORTIMER, *still pointing at* GIBBS, *goes around above table toward him.* GIBBS, *seeing a madman, rises slowly and backs toward* C., *then turns and runs for the exit* R., *with* MORTIMER *following him.* GIBBS *opens* R. *door and* MORTIMER *pushes him out, closing door after him. Then he turns and leans on door in exhausted relief. Meantime,* MARTHA *has risen and crossed to below armchair, while* ABBY *has risen and crossed to* D. C. (*If necessary to cover* GIBBS' *cross and exit,* MORTIMER *has the following lines . . . "Get out of here! Do you want to be poisoned? Do you want to be killed? Do you want to be murdered?"*). ABBY (*great disappointment*). Now you've spoiled everything. (*She goes to sofa and sits.*)

(MARTHA *sits in armchair.* MORTIMER *crosses to* C. *and looks from one to the other . . . then speaks to* ABBY.)

MORTIMER. You can't do things like that. I don't know how to explain this to you, but it's not only against the law. It's wrong! (*To* MARTHA.) It's not a nice thing to do. (MARTHA *turns away from him as* ABBY *has done in his lines to her.*) People wouldn't understand. (*Points to door after* GIBBS.) *He* wouldn't understand.

MARTHA. Abby, we shouldn't have told Mortimer!

MORTIMER. What I mean is—well, this has developed into a very bad habit.

ABBY (*rises*). Mortimer, we don't try to stop you from doing things you like to do. I don't see why you should interfere with us.

(*Phone rings.* MORTIMER *answers.* MARTHA *rises to below table.*)

MORTIMER. Hello! (*It's Al, again.*) All right, I'll see the first act and I'll pan the hell out of it. But look, Al, you've got to do something for me. Get hold of O'Brien—our lawyer, the head of our legal department. Have him meet me at the theatre. Now, don't let me down. O.K. I'm starting now. (*He hangs up and turns to* AUNTS.) Look, I've got to go to the theatre. I can't get out of it. But before I go will you promise me something?

MARTHA (*crossing to* ABBY *at* C.). We'd have to know what it was first.

MORTIMER. I love you very much and I know you love me. You know I'd do anything in the world for you and I want you to do just this little thing for me.

ABBY. What do you want us to do?

MORTIMER. Don't *do* anything. I mean don't do *anything.* Don't let any one in this house—and leave Mr. Hoskins right where he is.

MARTHA. Why?

MORTIMER. I want time to think—and I've got quite a little to think about. You know I wouldn't want anything to happen to you.

ABBY. Well, what on earth could happen to us?

MORTIMER (*beside himself*). Anyway—you'll do this for me, won't you?

MARTHA. Well—we were planning on holding services before dinner.

MORTIMER. Services!

MARTHA (*a little indignant*). Certainly. You don't think we'd bury Mr. Hoskins without a full Methodist service, do you? Why he was a Methodist.

MORTIMER. But can't that wait until I get back?

ABBY. Oh, then you could join us.

MORTIMER (*going crazy himself*). Yes! Yes!

ABBY. Oh, Mortimer, you'll enjoy the services—especially the hymns. (*To* MARTHA.) Remember how beautifully Mortimer use to sing in the choir before his voice changed?

MORTIMER. And remember, you're not going to let anyone in this house while I'm gone—it's a promise!

MARTHA. Well——

ABBY. Oh, Martha, we can do that now that Mortimer's co-operating with us. (*To Mortimer.*) Well, all right, Mortimer.

(MORTIMER *heaves a sigh of relief. Crosses to sofa and gets his hat. Then on his way to opening* R. *door, he speaks.*)

MORTIMER. Have you got some paper? I'll get back just a soon as I can. (*Taking legal papers from coat pocket as he crosses.*) There's a man I've got to see.

(ABBY *has gone to desk for stationery. She hands it to* MORTIMER.)

ABBY. Here's some stationery. Will this do?

MORTIMER (*taking stationery*). That'll be fine. I can save time if I write my review on the way to the theatre. (*He exits* R).

(*The two* AUNTS *stare after him.* MARTHA *crosses and closes door.* ABBY *goes to sideboard and brings two candelabra to table. Then gets matches from sideboard—lights candles during lines.*)

MARTHA. Mortimer didn't seem quite himself today.

ABBY (*lighting candles*). Well, that's only natural—I think I know why.

MARTHA (*lighting floor lamp*). Why?

ABBY. He's just become engaged to be married. I suppose that always makes a man nervous.

MARTHA (*during this speech she goes to first landing and closes curtains over windows, then comes downstairs and turns off remote switch*). Well, I'm so happy for Elaine—and their honeymoon ought to give Mortimer a real vacation. I don't think he got much rest this summer.

ABBY. Well, at least he didn't go kiting off to China or Spain.

MARTHA. I could never understand why he wanted to go to those places.

ABBY. Well, I think to Mortimer the theatre has always seemed pretty small potatoes. He needs something big to criticise— something like the human race. (*She sets one candelabra* D. L., *the other* U. R. *on table.*)

MARTHA (*at* C.). Oh, Abby, if Mortimer's coming back for the services for Mr. Hoskins, we'll need another hymnal. There's one in my room. (*She starts upstairs to first landing.*)

ABBY. You know, dear, it's really my turn to read the services, but since you weren't here when Mr. Hoskins came I want you to do it.

MARTHA (*pleased*). That's very nice of you, dear—but, are you sure you want me to?

ABBY. It's only fair.

MARTHA. Well, I think I'll wear my black bombazine and Mother's old brooch. (*She starts up again when door-bell rings.*)

ABBY (*crossing as far as desk*). I'll go, dear.

MARTHA (*hushed*). We promised Mortimer we wouldn't let anyone in.

ABBY (*trying to peer through curtained window in door*). Who do you suppose it is?

MARTHA. Wait a minute, I'll look. (*She turns to landing window and peeks out the curtains.*) It's two men—and I've never seen them before.

ABBY. Are you sure?

MARTHA. There's a car at the curb—they must have come in that.

ABBY. Let me look! (*She hurries upstairs. There is a knock on door. ABBY peeks out the curtains.*)

MARTHA. Do you recognise them?

ABBY. They're strangers to me.

MARTHA. We'll just have to pretend we're not home. (*The two of them huddle back in the corner of landing.*)

(*There is another knock at the door R., the knob is turned, and the door swings slowly open. A tall MAN walks to C., looking about the room. He walks in with assurance and ease as though the room were familiar to him—in every direction but that of the stairs. There is something sinister about the man—something that brings a slight chill in his presence. It is in his walk, his bearing, and his strange resemblance to Boris Karloff. From the stair-landing ABBY and MARTHA watch him, almost afraid to speak. Having completed his survey of the room, the MAN turns and addresses someone outside the front door.*)

JONATHAN. Come in, Doctor. (DR. EINSTEIN *enters R. He is somewhat ratty in appearance. His face wears the benevolent smirk of a man who lives in a pleasant haze of alcohol. There is something about him that suggests the unfrocked priest. He stands just inside the door, timid but expectant.*) This is the home of my youth. As a boy I couldn't wait to escape from this place—now I'm glad to escape back into it.

EINSTEIN (*shutting door. His back to AUNTS*). Yah, Chonny, it's a fine hideout.

JONATHAN. The family must still live here. There's something so unmistakably Brewster about the Brewsters. I hope there's a fatted calf awaiting the return of the prodigal.

EINSTEIN. Yah, I'm hungry. (*He suddenly sees the fatted calf in the form of the two glasses of wine on table.*) Look, Chonny, drinks! (*He runs over below to table. JONATHAN crosses to above side.*)

JONATHAN. As though we were expected. A good omen.

(*They raise glasses to their lips as* ABBY *steps down a couple of stairs and speaks.*)

ABBY. Who are you? What are you doing here! (*They both put glasses down.* EINSTEIN *picks up his hat from armchair, ready to run for it.* JONATHAN *turns to* ABBY.)

JONATHAN. Why, Aunt Abby! Aunt Martha! It's Jonathan.

MARTHA (*frightened*). You get out of here.

JONATHAN (*crossing to* AUNTS). I'm Jonathan—your nephew, Jonathan.

ABBY. Oh, no, you're not. You're nothing like Jonathan, so don't pretend you are! You just get out of here!

JONATHAN (*crossing closer*). But I am Jonathan. And this (*indicating* EINSTEIN) is Dr. Einstein.

ABBY. And he's not Dr. Einstein either.

JONATHAN. Not Dr. Albert Einstein—Dr. Herman Einstein.

ABBY (*down another step*). Who are you? You're not our nephew, Jonathan.

JONATHAN (*peering at* ABBY'S *outstretched hand*). I see you're still wearing the lovely garnet ring that Grandma Brewster bought in England. (ABBY *gasps, looks at ring.*) And you, Aunt Martha, still the high collar—to hide the scar where Grandfather's acid burned you. (MARTHA'S *hand goes to her throat. The two* AUNTS *look at* JONATHAN. MARTHA *comes down a few steps behind* ABBY. EINSTEIN *gets to* C.).

MARTHA. His voice is like Jonathan's.

ABBY (*stepping down to stage floor*). Have you been in an accident?

JONATHAN (*his hand goes to side of his face*). No—(*He clouds*)—my face—Dr. Einstein is responsible for that. He's a plastic surgeon. He changes people's faces.

MARTHA (*comes down to* ABBY). But I've seen that face before. (*To* ABBY). Abby, remember when we took the little Schultz boy to the movies and I was so frightened? It was that face!

(JONATHAN *grows tense and looks toward* EINSTEIN. EINSTEIN *crosses to* C. *and addresses* AUNTS).

EINSTEIN. Easy, Chonny—easy! (*To* AUNTS .) Don't worry ladies. The last five years I give Chonny three new faces. I give him another one right away. This last face—well, I saw that picture too—just before I operate. And I was intoxicated.

JONATHAN (*with a growing and dangerous intensity as he walks toward* EINSTEIN, *who backs* D. S.). You see, Doctor—you see what you've done to me. Even my own family——

EINSTEIN (*to calm him, as he is forced around* R. *stage*). Chonny— you're home—in this lovely house—— (*To* AUNTS.) How often he tells me about Brooklyn—about this house—about his aunts that he lofes so much. (*To* JONATHAN.) They know you, Chonny. (*To* ABBY *as he leads her toward* JONATHAN.) You know it's Jonathan. Speak to him. Tell him so. (*He drifts above table to* D. L. *of it.*)

ABBY. Well—Jonathan—it's been a long time—what have you been doing all these years?

MARTHA (*has come to far* D. R.). Yes, Jonathan, where have you been?

JONATHAN (*recovering his composure*). Oh, England, South Africa, Australia,—the last five years Chicago. Dr. Einstein and I were in business there together.

ABBY. Oh, we were in Chicago for the World's Fair.

MARTHA (*for want of something to say*). Yes—we found Chicago awfully warm.

EINSTEIN (*he has wandered above* U. L. *and down to below table.*) Yah—it got hot for us too.

JONATHAN (*turning on the charm as he crosses above* ABBY, *placing himself between the two* AUNTS.) Well, it's wonderful to be in Brooklyn again. And you—Abby—Martha you don't look a day older. Just as I remembered you—sweet—charming—hospitable. (*The* AUNTS *don't react too well to this charm.*) And dear Teddy—(*he indicates with his hand a lad of eight or ten*)—did he get into politics? (*He turns to* EINSTEIN.) My little brother, Doctor, was determined to become President.

ABBY. Oh, Teddy's fine! Just fine! And Mortimer's well too.

JONATHAN (*a bit of a sneer*). I know about Mortimer. I've seen his picture at the head of his column. He's evidently fulfilled all the promise of his early nasty nature.

ABBY (*defensively*). We're very fond of Mortimer.

(*There is a slight pause. Then* MARTHA *speaks uneasily as she gestures toward* R. *door.*)

MARTHA. Well, Jonathan, it's very nice to have seen you again.

JONATHAN (*expanding*). Bless you, Aunt Martha. (*Crosses and sits chair* R. *of table.*) It's good to be home again.

(*The two* AUNTS *look at each other with dismay.*)

ABBY. Well, Martha, we mustn't let what's on the stove boil over. (*She starts to kitchen, then sees* MARTHA *isn't following. She crosses back and tugs at* MARTHA, *then crosses toward kitchen again.* MARTHA *follows to* C., *then speaks to* JONATHAN.)

MARTHA. Yes. If you'll excuse us for a minute, Jonathan. Unless you're in a hurry to go somewhere.

(JONATHAN *looks at her balefully.* MARTHA *crosses around above table, takes bottle of wine and puts it back in sideboard, then exits with* ABBY. ABBY, *who has been waiting in kitchen doorway for* MARTHA, *closes door after them.* EINSTEIN *crosses* U. L. *around to behind* JONATHAN.)

EINSTEIN.. Well, Chonny, where do we go from here? We got to think fast. The police. The police have got pictures of that face. I got to operate on you right away. We got to find some place for that—and we got to find a place for Mr. Spenalzo too.

JONATHA. Don't waste any worry on that rat.

EINSTEIN. But, Chonny, we got a hot stiff on our hands.

JONATHAN (*flinging hat on to sofa.*) Forget Mr. Spenalzo!

EINSTEIN. But you can't leave a dead body in the rumble seat. You shouldn't have killed him, Chonny. He's a nice fellow—he gives us a lift—and what happens?

JONATHAN (*remembering bitterly*). He said I looked like Boris Karloff! (*He starts for* EINSTEIN.) That's your work, Doctor. You did that to me!

EINSTEIN (*he's backed away to* D. L. *of table*). Now, Chonny—we find a place somewhere—I fix you up quick!

JONATHAN. Tonight!

EINSTEIN. Chonny—I got to eat first. I'm hungry—I'm weak.

(*The* AUNTS *enter from kitchen. Abby comes to* JONATHAN *at* C. MARTHA *remains in kitchen doorway.*)

ABBY. Jonathan—we're glad that you remembered us and took the trouble to come in and say "Hello." But you were never happy in this house and we were never happy while you were in it—so, we've just come in to say goodbye.

JONATHAN (*takes a menacing step toward* ABBY. *Then decides to try the "charm" again*). Aunt Abby, I can't say that your feeling toward me comes as a surprise. I've spent a great many hours regretting the many heartaches I must have given you as a boy.

ABBY. You were quite a trial to us, Jonathan.

JONATHAN. But my great disappointment is for Dr. Einstein. (EINSTEIN *is a little surprised.*) I promised him that no matter how rushed we were in passing through Brooklyn, I'd take the time to bring him here for one of Aunt Martha's home-cooked dinners.

(MARTHA *rises to this a bit, stepping* D. S.).

MARTHA. Oh . . .

ABBY (*backing* U. L.). I'm sorry. I'm afraid there wouldn't be enough.

MARTHA. Abby, it's a pretty good sized pot roast.

JONATHAN (*how wonderful*). Pot roast!

MARTHA. I think the least we can do is to——

JONATHAN. Thank you, Aunt Martha! We'll stay to dinner.

ABBY (*backing to kitchen door and not at all pleased*). Well, we'll hurry it along.

MARTHA. Yes! (*She exits into kitchen.*)

ABBY (*stopping in doorway*). Oh, Jonathan, if you want to freshen up—why don't you use the washroom in Grandfather's old laboratory?

JONATHAN (*crossing to her*). Is that still there?

ABBY. Oh, yes. Just as he left it. Well, I'll help Martha get things started—since we're all in a hurry. (*She exits into kitchen.*)

EINSTEIN (*stepping* U. S.). Well, we get a meal anyway.

JONATHAN (*above table*). Grandfather's laboratory! (*Looks upstairs.*) And just as it was. Doctor, a perfect operating room.

EINSTEIN. Too bad we can't use it.

JONATHAN. After you'd finished with me—— Why, we could make a fortune here. The laboratory—that large ward in the attic—ten beds, Doctor—and Brooklyn is crying for your talents.

EINSTEIN. Vy vork yourself up, Chonny? Anyway, for Brooklyn I think we're a year too late.

JONATHAN. You don't know this town, Doctor. Practically everybody in Brooklyn needs a new face.

EINSTEIN. But so many of the old faces are locked up.

JONATHAN. A very small percentage—and the boys in Brooklyn are famous for paying generously to stay out of jail.

EINSTEIN. Take it easy, Chonny. Your aunts—they don't want us here.

JONATHAN. We're here for dinner, aren't we?

EINSTEIN. Yah—but after dinner?

JONATHAN (*crossing up to sofa*). Leave it to me, Doctor. I'll handle it. Why, this house'll be our headquarters for years.

EINSTEIN (*a pretty picture*). Oh, that would be beautiful, Chonny! This nice quiet house. Those aunts of yours—what sweet ladies. I love them already. I get the bags, yah?

JONATHAN (*stopping him.*) Doctor! We must wait until we're invited.

EINSTEIN. But you chust said that——

JONATHAN. We'll be invited.

EINSTEIN. And if they say no——?

JONATHAN. Doctor—two helpless old women——? (*He sits on sofa.*)

EINSTEIN (*takes bottle flask from hip pocket and unscrews cork as he crosses to window-seat*). It's like comes true a beautiful dream—— Only I hope you're not dreaming. (*He stretches out on window-seat, taking a swig from bottle.*) It's so peaceful.

JONATHAN (*stretched out of sofa*). That's what makes this house so perfect for us—it's so peaceful.

(TEDDY *enters from cellar, blows a terrific blast on his bugle, as* JONATHAN *backs* R. TEDDY *marches to stairs and on up to first landing as the two* MEN *look at his tropical garb with some astonishment.*)

TEDDY. CHARGE! (*He rushes up the stairs and off.*)

(JONATHAN *watches him from foot of stairs.* EINSTEIN, *sitting on window-seat, takes a hasty swig from his flask as the curtain comes down on the word CHARGE!*).

ACT TWO

SCENE: *The same. Later that night.* JONATHAN, *with an after-dinner cigar, is occupying armchair at* L. *of table, completely at his ease.* ABBY *and* MARTHA, *seated on window-seat, are giving him a nervous attention in the attitude of people who wish their guests would go home.* EINSTEIN *is relaxed and happy in the chair* R. *of table. The dinner dishes have been cleared. There is a red cloth on the table, with a saucer to serve as an ash-try for* JONATHAN. *The room is in order. All doors are closed, as are the curtains over the windows.*

JONATHAN. Yes, Aunties, those five years in Chicago were amongst the busiest and happiest of my life.

EINSTEIN. And from Chicago we go to South Bend, Indiana. (*He shakes his head as though he wishes they hadn't.*)

(JONATHAN *give him a look.*)

JONATHAN. They wouldn't be interested in our experience in Indiana.

ABBY. Well, Jonathan, you've led a very interesting life, I'm sure—but we really shouldn't have allowed you to talk so late. (*She starts to rise.* JONATHAN *seats her just by the tone of this voice.*)

JONATHAN. My meeting Dr. Einstein in London, I might say, changed the whole course of my life. You remember I had been in South Africa, in the diamond business—then Amsterdam, the diamond market. I wanted to go back to South Africa—and Dr. Einstein made it possible for me.

EINSTEIN. A good job, Chonny. (*To* AUNTS.) When we take off the bandages—his face looked so different, the nurse had to introduce me.

JONATHAN. I loved that face. I still carry the picture with me. (*He produces a snapshot-size picture from his inside coat pocket, looks at it a moment, then hands it to* MARTHA. *She looks at it and hands it to* ABBY).

ABBY. This looks more the way you used to look, but still I wouldn't know you.

JONATHAN. I think we'll go back to that face, Doctor.

EINSTEIN. Yah, it's safe now.

ABBY (*rising*). Well, I know you both want to get to—where you're going.

JONATHAN (*relaxing even more*). My dear aunts—I'm so full of that delicious dinner I'm unable to move a muscle.

EINSTEIN (*relaxing too*). Yah, it's nice here.

MARTHA (*rises*). After all—it's very late and——

(TEDDY *enters on balcony wearing his solar topee, carrying a book, open, and another solar topee.*)

TEDDY (*descending stairs*). I found it! I found it!

JONATHAN. What did you find, Teddy?

TEDDY. The story of my life—my biography. (*He crosses above to* L. *of* EINSTEIN.) Here's the picture I was telling you about, General (*He lays open book on table showing picture to* EINSTEIN.) Here we are, both of us. "President Roosevelt and General Goethals at Culebra Cut." That's me, General, and that's you.

(EINSTEIN *looks at picture.*)

EINSTEIN. My, how I've changed.

(TEDDY *looks at Einstein, a little puzzled, but makes the adjustment.*)

TEDDY. Well, you see that picture hasn't been taken yet. We haven't even started work on Culebra Cut. We're still digging locks. And now, General, we will both go to Panama and inspect the new lock. (*Hands him solar topee.*)

ABBY. No, Teddy—not to Panama.

EINSTEIN. We go some other time. Panama's a long way off.

TEDDY. Nonsense, it's just down in the cellar.

JONATHAN. The cellar?

MARTHA. We let him dig the Panama Canal in the cellar.

TEDDY (*severely*). General Goethals, as President of the United States, Commander-in-Chief of the Army and Navy and the man who gave you this job, I demand that you accompany me on the inspection of the new lock.

JONATHAN. Teddy! I think it's time you went to bed.

TEDDY. I beg your pardon! (*He crosses above to* L. *of* JONATHAN, *putting on his pince-nez as he crosses.*) Who are you?

JONATHAN. I'm Woodrow Wilson. Go to bed.

TEDDY. No—you're not Wilson. But your face is familiar. Let me see——You're not any one I know now. Perhaps later—— On my hunting trip of Africa—yes, you look like someone I might meet in the jungle.

(JONATHAN *stiffens.* ABBY *crosses in front of* TEDDY, *getting between him and* JONATHAN.)

ABBY. It's your brother, Jonathan, dear.

MARTHA (*rising*). He's had his face changed.

TEDDY. So that's it—a nature faker!

ABBY. And perhaps you had better go to bed, Teddy—Jonathan and his friend have to go back to their hotel.

JONATHAN (*rising*). General Goethals (*to* EINSTEIN), inspect the canal. (*He crosses to* U. C.).

EINSTEIN (*rising.*) All right, Mr. President. We go to Panama.

TEDDY. Bully! Bully! (*He crosses to cellar door, opens it.*) Follow me, General. (EINSTEIN *goes up to* L. *of* TEDDY. TEDDY *taps solar topee in* EINSTEINS'S *hand, then taps his own head.*) It's down south you know. (*He exits downstairs.*)

(EINSTEIN *puts on solar topee, which is too large for him. Then turns in cellar doorway and speaks.*)

EINSTEIN. Well—bon voyage. (*He exits, closing door.*)

JONATHAN. Aunt Abby, I must correct your misapprehension. You spoke of our hotel. We have no hotel. We came directly here——

MARTHA. Well, there's a very nice little hotel just three blocks down the——

JONATHAN (*cutting her off*). Aunt Martha, this is my home.

ABBY. But, Jonathan, you can't stay here. We need our rooms.

JONATHAN. You need them?

ABBY. Yes, for our lodgers.

JONATHAN. (*alarmed*). Are there lodgers in this house?

MARTHA. Well, not just now, but we plan to have some.

JONATHAN (*cutting her off again*). Then my old room is still free.

ABBY. But, Jonathan, there's no place for Dr. Einstein.

JONATHAN (*crosses below table, drops cigar ashes into saucer*). He'll share the room with me.

ABBY. No, Jonathan, I'm afraid you can't stay here.

(JONATHAN *is below table. He grinds cigar out in saucer, then starts towards the* AUNTS. *The* AUNTS *back around above table to* C., MARTHA *first.* JONATHAN *turns back and crosses below table to* ABBY *at* C.).

JONATHAN. Dr. Einstein and I need a place to sleep. You remembered, this afternoon, that as a boy I could be disagreeable. It wouldn't be very pleasant for any of us if——

MARTHA (R. C., *and frightened*). Perhaps we'd better let them stay here tonight——

ABBY. Well, just overnight, Jonathan.

JONATHAN. That's settled. Now, if you'll get my room ready——

MARTHA (*starting upstairs,* ABBY *following*). It only needs airing out.

ABBY. We keep it ready to show our lodgers. I think you and Dr. Einstein will find it comfortable.

(JONATHAN *follows them to first balcony and leans on newel-post.* AUNTS *are on the balcony.*)

JONATHAN. You have a most distinguished guest in Dr. Einstein. I'm afraid you don't appreciate his skill. But you will. In a few weeks you'll see me looking like a very different Jonathan.

MARTHA. He can't operate on you here.

JONATHAN (*ignoring*). When Dr. Einstein and I get organised— when we resume practice—Oh, I forgot to tell you. We're turning Grandfather's laboratory into an operating room. We expect to be quite busy.

ABBY. Jonathan, we will not let you turn this house into a hospital.

JONATHAN (*laughing*). A hospital—heavens no! It will be a beauty parlour.

(EINSTEIN *enters excitedly from cellar.*)

EINSTEIN. Hey, Chonny, down in the cellar——(*He sees* AUNTS *and stops.*)

JONATHAN. Dr. Einstein—my dear aunts have invited us to live with them.

EINSTEIN. Oh, you fixed it?

ABBY. Well, you're sleeping here tonight.

JONATHAN. Please get our room ready immediately.

MARTHA. Well——

ABBY. For tonight.

(*They exit through arch.* JONATHAN *comes to foot of stairs.*)

EINSTEIN. Chonny, when I go down in the cellar, what do you think I find?

JONATHAN. What?

EINSTEIN. The Panama Canal.

JONATHAN (*disgusted, crossing to* C.). The Panama Canal.

EINSTEIN. It just fits Mr. Spenalzo. It's a hole Teddy dug. Six feet long and four feet wide.

JONATHAN (*gets the idea. Opens cellar door and looks down.*) Down there!

EINSTEIN. You'd think they knew we were bringing Mr. Spenalzo along. That's hospitality.

JONATHAN (*closing cellar door*). Rather a good joke on my aunts— their living in a house with a body buried in the cellar.

EINSTEIN. How do we get him in?

JONATHAN (*drops* D. S.). Yes. We can't just walk him through the door. (*He sees window in* L. *wall.*) We'll drive the car up between the house and the cemetery—then when they've gone to bed, we'll bring Mr. Spenalzo in through the window.

EINSTEIN (*taking out bottle flask*). Bed! Just think, we got a bed tonight! (*He starts swigging.*)

JONATHAN (*grabbing his arm*). Easy, Doctor. Remember you're operating tomorrow. And this time you'd better be sober.

EINSTEIN. I fix you up beautiful.

JONATHAN. And if you don't——(*Gives* EINSTEIN *shove to door.*)

ABBY (*she and* MARTHA *enter on balcony*). Jonathan! Your room is ready.

JONATHAN. Then you can go to bed. We're moving the car up behind the house.

MARTHA. It's all right where it is—until morning.

JONATHAN (EINSTEIN *has opened door*). I don't want to leave it in the street—that might be against the law. (*He exits.*)

(EINSTEIN *follows him out, closing door.* ABBY *and* MARTHA *start downstairs and reach below table.*)

MARTHA. Abby, what are we going to do?

ABBY. Well, we're not going to let them stay more than one night in this house for one thing. What would the neighbours think? People coming in here with one face and going out with another. (*She has reached table* D. S. MARTHA *is at her* R.).

MARTHA. What are we going to do about Mr. Hoskins?

ABBY (*crosses to window-seat.* MARTHA *follows*). Oh, Mr. Hoskins. It can't be very comfortable for him in there. And he's been so patient, the poor dear. Well, I think Teddy had better get Mr. Hoskins downstairs right away.

MARTHA (*adamant*). Abby—I will not invite Jonathan to the funeral services.

ABBY. Oh, no. We'll wait until they're gone to bed and then come down and hold the services.

(TEDDY *enters from cellar, gets book from table and starts* R. ABBY *stops him at* C.).

TEDDY. General Goethals was very pleased. He says the Canal is just the right size.

ABBY (*crosses to* C.). Teddy! Teddy, there's been another Yellow Fever victim.

TEDDY (*takes off pince-nez*). Dear me—this will be a shock to the General.

MARTHA (*stepping* R.). Then we mustn't tell him about it.

TEDDY (*crosses below* ABBY *to* MARTHA). But it's his department.

ABBY. No, we mustn't tell him Teddy. It would just spoil his visit.

TEDDY. I'm sorry, Aunt Abby. It's out of my hands—he'll have to be told. Army regulations, you know.

ABBY. No, Teddy, we *must* keep it a secret.

MARTHA. Yes!

TEDDY (*he loves them*). A state secret?

ABBY. Yes, a state secret?

MARTHA. Promise?

TEDDY (*what a silly request*). You have the word of the President of the United States. (*Crosses his heart.*) Cross my heart and hope to die. (*He spits.*) Now let's see—(*puts pince-nez on, then puts arms around both* AUNTS) how are we going to keep it a secret?

ABBY. Well, Teddy, you go back down in the cellar and when I turn out the lights—when it's all dark—you come up and take the poor man down to the Canal. (*Urging him to cellar door, which he opens.*) Now go along, Teddy.

MARTHA (*following* U. S.). And we'll come down later and hold services.

TEDDY (*in doorway*). You may announce the President will say a few words. (*He starts, then turns back.*) Where is the poor devil?

MARTHA. He's in the window-seat.

TEDDY. It seems to be spreading. We've never had Yellow Fever there before. (*He exits, closing door.*)

ABBY. Martha, when Jonathan and Dr. Einstein come back, let's see if we can get them to go to bed right away.

MARTHA. Yes. Then by the time they're asleep, we'll be dressed for the funeral. (*Sudden thought.*) Abby, I've never even seen Mr. Hoskins.

ABBY. Oh, my goodness, that's right—you were out. Well, you just come right over and see his now. (*They go to window-seat, ABBY first.*) He's really very nice looking—considering he's a Methodist. (*As they go to lift window-seat, JONATHAN throws window open from outside with a bang. The AUNTS scream and draw back. JONATHAN puts his head in through curtains.*)

JONATHAN. We're bringing—the luggage through here.

ABBY (*now at C.*). Jonathan, your room's waiting for you. You can go right up.

(*Two dusty bags and a large instrument case are passed through window by EINSTEIN, JONATHAN puts them on floor.*)

JONATHAN. I'm afraid we don't keep Brooklyn hours—but you two run along to bed.

ABBY. Now, you must be very tired, both of you—and we don't go to bed this early.

JONATHAN. Well, you should. It's time I came home to take care of you.

MARTHA. We weren't planning to go until——

JONATHAN (*the master*). Aunt Martha, did you hear me say go to bed! (*AUNT MARTHA starts upstairs as EINSTEIN comes in through window and picks up two bags. JONATHAN takes instrument case and puts it U. S. of window-seat.*) The instruments can go to the laboratory in the morning. (*EINSTEIN starts upstairs. JONATHAN closes window. MARTHA is part way upstairs as EINSTEIN passes her. ABBY is at R. C.*). Now then we're all going to bed. (*He crosses to C. as ABBY breaks D. R. to light-switch.*)

ABBY. I'll wait till you're up, then turn out the lights.

(*JONATHAN, going upstairs, sees EINSTEIN pausing at balcony door. MARTHA is almost up to balcony.*)

JONATHAN. Another flight, Doctor. (*To Martha.*) Run along, Aunt Martha. (*MARTHA hurries into doorway. EINSTEIN goes through arch to third floor. JONATHAN continues on to L. end of balcony. ABBY is at light-switch.*) All right, Aunt Abby.

ABBY (*stalling. Looks toward cellar door*). I'll be right up.

JONATHAN. Now, Aunt Abby. (*Definite.*) Turn out the lights!

(*ABBY turns switch, plunging stage into darkness except for spot shining down stairway from arch. ABBY goes upstairs to her door where*

MARTHA *is waiting. She takes a last frightened look at* JONATHAN *and exits.* MARTHA *closes door.* JONATHAN *goes off through arch, closing that door, blotting out the spot. A street light shines through main door* R. *on stage floor.* TEDDY *opens cellar door, then turns on cellar light, outlining him in the doorway. He crosses to window-seat and opens it—the window-seat cover giving out its usual rusty squeak, He reaches in and pulls Mr. Hoskins (a live "dummy" light enough to carry and who can remain stiff as in rigor mortis.) He gets Mr. Hoskins over his shoulder and, leaving window open, crosses to cellar door and goes down into cellar with Mr. Hoskins. Closes door.* JONATHAN *and* EINSTEIN *come through arch. It is dark. They light matches and listen at the* AUNT'S *door for a moment.* EINSTEIN *speaks.*)

EINSTEIN. All right, Chonny.

(*The matches go out.* JONATHAN *lights another and they come down to foot of stairs.*)

JONATHAN. I'll get the window open. You go round and hand him through.

EINSTEIN. No, he's too heavy for me. You go outside and push—I stay here and pull. Then together we get him down to Panama.

JONATHAN. All right. (*He blows out match, crosses and opens door.* EINSTEIN *to his* L.). I'll take a look around outside the house. When I tap on the glass you open the window.

EINSTEIN. All right. (JONATHAN *exits, closing door.* EINSTEIN *lights match and crosses* L. *He bumps into table and match goes out. He feels his way* L. *from there. We hear ejaculations and noise.* EINSTEIN *has fallen into window-seat. In window-seat he lights another match and slowly rises up to a sitting position and looks around. He blows out match and hauls himself out of window-seat, speaking the while.*) Who left dis open? Dummkopf! (*We hear the creak of the cover as he closes it. In the darkness we hear a tap on* L. *window.* EINSTEIN *opens it. Then in a hushed voice.*) Chonny? O.K. Allez Oop. Wait—wait a minute. You lost a leg somewhere.—Ach—now I got him. Come on—ugh——(*He falls on floor and there is a crash of a body and the sound of a "Sshhhh" from outside.*) That was me, Chonny. I schlipped.

JONATHAN (*voice*). Be more careful.

(*Pause.*)

EINSTEIN. Well, his shoe came off. (*Pause.*) All right, Chonny. I got him! (*There is a knock at* R. *door.*) Chonny! Somebody at the door! Go quick. NO. I manage here—go quick!

(*There is a second knock at the door. A moment's silence and we hear the creak of the window-seat as* EINSTEIN *puts Mr. Spenalzo in Mr. Hoskins' place. There is a third knock, as* EINSTEIN *struggles with the body. A fourth knock and then the creak of the window-seat as* EINSTEIN *closes it. He scrurries around to beside desk, keeping low to avoid being seen through door.* ELAINE *enters* R., *calling softly.*)

ELAINE. Miss Abby! Miss Martha! (*In the dim path of light she comes toward* C., *calling toward balcony.*) Miss Abby! Miss Martha! (*Suddenly* JONATHAN *steps through door and closes it. The noise swings* ELAINE *around and she gasps.*) Uhhh! Who is it? Is that you, Teddy? (JONATHAN *comes toward her as he backs into chair* R. *of table.*) Who are you?

JONATHAN. Who are *you?*

ELAINE. I'm Elaine Harper—I live next door!

JONATHAN. Then what are you doing here?

ELAINE. I came over to see Miss Abby and Miss Martha.

JONATHAN (*to* EINSTEIN, *without turning.* EINSTEIN *has crept to light-switch after* JONATHAN'S *cross*). Turn on the lights, Doctor. (*The lights go on,* ELAINE *gasps as she sees* JONATHAN *and sits in chair.* JONATHAN *looks at her for a moment.*) You chose rather an untimely moment for a social call. (*He crosses toward window-seat, looking for Spenalzo, but doesn't see him. He looks up, behind table. Looks out window, then comes back into the room.*)

ELAINE (*trying to summon courage*). I think you'd better explain what *you're* doing here.

JONATHAN (D. L. *of table*). We happen to live here.

ELAINE. You *don't* live here. I'm in this house every day and I've never seen you before. (*Frightened.*) Where are Miss Abby and Miss Martha? What have you done to them?

JONATHAN (*a step to below table*). Perhaps we'd better introduce ourselves. This—(*indicating*)—is Dr. Einstein.

ELAINE (*looks at* EINSTEIN). Dr. Einstein? (*Shes turns back to* JONATHAN. EINSTEIN, *behind her back, is gesturing to* JONATHAN *the whereabouts of Spenalzo.*)

JONATHAN. A surgeon of great distinction—(*he looks under table for Spenalzo, and not finding him*—)—and something of a magician.

ELAINE. And I suppose you're going to tell me you're Boris Kar——

JONATHAN. I'm Jonathan Brewster.

ELAINE (*drawing back almost with fright*). Oh—you're Jonathan!

JONATHAN. I see you've heard of me.

(EINSTEIN *drifts to front of sofa.*)

ELAINE. Yes—just this afternoon for the first time.

JONATHAN (*stepping toward her*). And what did they say about me?

ELAINE. Only that there was another brother named Jonathan— that's all that was said. (*Calming.*) Well, that explains everything. Now that I know who you are—(*running to* R. *door*). I'll be running along back home. (*The door is locked. She turns to* JONATHAN.) If you'll kindly unlock the door.

(JONATHAN *crosses to her, then before reaching her, he turns* D. S. *to* R. *door and unlocks it.* EINSTEIN *drifts down to chair* R. *of table. As* JONATHAN *opens door part way,* ELAINE *starts toward it. He turns and stops her with a gesture.*)

JONATHAN. "That explains everything"? Just what did you mean by that? Why did you come here at this time of night?

ELAINE. I thought I saw someone prowling around the house. I suppose it was you.

(JONATHAN *closes door and locks it, leaving key in lock.*)

JONATHAN. You thought you saw someone prowling around the house?

ELAINE. Yes—weren't you outside? Isn't that your car?

JONATHAN. You saw someone at the car?

ELAINE. Yes.

JONATHAN (*coming toward her as she backs* U. L.). What else did you see?

ELAINE. Just someone walking around the house to the car.

JONATHAN. What else did you see?

ELAINE. Just that—that's all. That's why I came over here. I wanted to tell Miss Abby to call the police. But if it was you, and that's your car, I don't need to bother Miss Abby. I'll be running along. (*She takes a step toward door above* JONATHAN. *He steps in her path.*)

JONATHAN. What was the man doing at the car?

ELAINE (*excited*). I don't know. You see I was on my way over here.

JONATHAN (*forcing her as she backs* L.). I think you're lying.

EINSTEIN (*crosses to* U. R. C.). I think she tells the truth, Chonny. We let her go now, huh?

JONATHAN (*still forcing her* L.). I think she's lying. Breaking into a house this time of night. I think she's dangerous. She shouldn't be allowed around loose. (*He seizes* ELAINE'S *arm. She screams.*)

ELAINE. Take your hands off me——

JONATHAN. Doctor——

(*As* EINSTEIN *starts* L., TEDDY *enters from cellar, shutting door. He looks at* JONATHAN L., *then speaks to* EINSTEIN R.).

TEDDY (*simply*). It's going to be a private funeral. (*He goes upstairs to first landing.* ELAINE *crosses to desk, dragging* JONATHAN *with her.*)

ELAINE. Teddy! Teddy! Tell these men who I am!

(TEDDY *turns and looks at her.*)

TEDDY. That's my daughter—Alice. (*He cries* "CHARGE!" *Dashes upstairs and exits.*)

ELAINE (*struggling to get away from* JONATHAN *and dragging him to* R. C.) No! No! Teddy!

(JONATHAN *has* ELAINE'S *arm twisted in back of her, his other hand is over her mouth.*)

JONATHAN. Doctor! Your handkerchief! (*As* EINSTEIN *hands him a handkerchief,* JONATHAN *releases his hand from* ELAINE'S *mouth to take it. She screams. He puts his hand over her mouth again. Spies the cellar door and speaks to* EINSTEIN.) The cellar!

IVERPOOL JOHN MOORES UNIVERSITY
LEARNING SERVICES

(EINSTEIN *runs and opens cellar door. (Cellar light is on). Then he runs back and turns off light-switch, putting stage in darkness.* JONATHAN *pushes* ELAINE *through cellar doorway,* EINSTEIN *runs back and down cellar stairs with* ELAINE. JONATHAN *shuts door, remaining on stage as the* AUNTS *enter on balcony above in their mourning clothes. Everything is in complete darkness except for the street lamp.*)

ABBY. What's the matter?

MARTHA. What's happening down there? (MARTHA *shuts her door and* ABBY *puts on lights from switch on balcony. They look down at the room a moment, then come downstairs, speaking as they come.*)

ABBY. What's the matter? (*Reaching foot of stairs as she sees* JONATHAN). What are you doing?

JONATHAN. We caught a burglar—a sneak thief. Go back to your room.

ABBY. We'll call the police.

JONATHAN. We've called the police. We'll handle this. Go back to your room. Do you hear me?

(*The door-bell rings, followed by several knocks.* ABBY *runs and opens* R. *door.* MORTIMER *enters with suitcase. At the same time,* ELAINE *runs out of cellar and into* MORTIMER'S *arms.* JONATHAN *makes a grab for* ELAINE *but misses. This leaves him* D. S. C. EINSTEIN *sneaks to* D. S. *behind* JONATHAN.)

ELAINE. Mortimer! (*He drops suitcase.*) Where have you been?

MORTIMER. To the Nora Bayes Theatre and I should have known better. (*He sees* JONATHAN.) My God!—I'm still there.

(ABBY *is at* R. *of* MORTIMER.)

ABBY. This is your brother Jonathan—and this is Dr. Einstein.

(MORTIMER *surveys his* AUNTS *all dressed in black.*)

MORTIMER. I know this isn't a nightmare, but what is it?

JONATHAN. I've come back home, Mortimer.

MORTIMER (*looking at him, and then to* ABBY). Who did you say this was?

ABBY. It's your brother Jonathan. He's had his face changed. Dr. Einstein performed the operation.

MORTIMER (*taking a closer look at* JONATHAN). Jonathan! Jonathan, you always were a horror, but do you have to look like one?

(JONATHAN *takes a step toward him.* EINSTEIN *pulls on his sleeve.* ELAINE *and* MARTHA *draw back to desk.*)

EINSTEIN. Easy, Chonny! Easy.

JONATHAN. Mortimer, have you forgotten the things I used to do to you when we were boys? Remember the time you were tied to the bedpost—the needles under your fingernails——?

MORTIMER. By God, it is Jonathan.—Yes, I remember. I remember you as the most detestable, vicious, venomous form of animal life I ever knew.

(JONATHAN *grows tense.* ABBY *steps between them.*)

ABBY. Now don't you two boys start quarrelling again the minute you've seen each other.

MORTIMER (*crosses to door, opens it*). There won't be any fight, Aunt Abby. Jonathan, you're not wanted here—get out!

JONATHAN. Dr. Einstein and I have been invited to stay.

MORTIMER. Not in this house.

ABBY. Just for tonight.

MORTIMER. I don't want him anywhere near me.

ABBY. But we did invite them for tonight, and it wouldn't be very nice to go back on our word.

MORTIMER (*unwillingly*). All right, tonight. But the first thing in the morning—out! (*He picks up his suitcase.*) Where are they sleeping?

ABBY. We put them in Jonathan's old room.

MORTIMER. That's my old room. (*Starts upstairs.*) I'm sleeping in that room. I'm here to stay.

MARTHA. Oh, Mortimer, I'm so glad.

EINSTEIN. Chonny, we sleep down here.

MORTIMER. You bet your life you sleep down here.

EINSTEIN (*to* JONATHAN). You sleep on the sofa and I sleep on the window-seat.

(*At the mention of window-seat,* MORTIMER *has reached the landing; after hanging his hat on hall tree, he turns and comes slowly downstairs, speaking as he reaches the floor and crossing over to window-seat. He drops back at* U. S. *end of window-seat.*)

MORTIMER. The window-seat! Oh, well, let's not argue about it. That window-seat's good enough for me for tonight. I'll sleep on the window-seat. (*As* MORTIMER *crosses above table,* EINSTEIN *makes a gesture as though to stop him from going to window-seat, but he's too late. He turns to* JONATHAN *as* MORTIMER *sits on window-seat.*)

EINSTEIN. You know, Chonny—all this argument—it makes me think of Mr. Spenalzo.

JONATHAN. Spenalzo! (*He steps* U. S. *looking around for Spenalzo again. Realising it would be best for them to remain downstairs, he speaks to* MORTIMER.) Well, now, Mortimer—— It really isn't necessary to inconvenience you like this—we'll sleep down here.

MORTIMER (*rising*). Jonathan, your sudden consideration for me is very unconvincing.

EINSTEIN (*goes upstairs to landing*). Come along, Chonny. We get our things out of the room, eh?

MORTIMER. Don't bother, Doctor!

JONATHAN. By the way, Doctor, I've completely lost track of Mr. Spenalzo.

MORTIMER. Who's this Mr. Spenalzo?

EINSTEIN (*from landing*). Just a friend of ours Chonny's been looking for.

MORTIMER. Well, don't bring anyone else in here!

EINSTEIN. It's all right, Chonny. While we pack I tell you all about it. (*He goes on up and through arch.* JONATHAN *starts upstairs.*)

ABBY (*dropping* D. S). Mortimer, you don't have to sleep down here. I can go in with Martha and you can take my room.

JONATHAN (*he has reached the balcony*). No trouble at all, Aunt Abby. We'll be packed in a few minutes. And then you can have the room, Mortimer. (*He exits through arch.*)

(MORTIMER *crosses up to sofa.* MARTHA *crosses to above armchair at* L. *of table and as* MORTIMER *speaks she picks up sport shoe belonging to*

Spenalzo, that EINSTEIN *puts there in blackout scene, unnoticed by anyone. She pretends to dust hem of her dress.*)

MORTIMER. You're just wasting your time—I told you I'm sleeping down here.

(ELAINE *leaps up from stool into* MORTIMER'S *arms.*)

ELAINE. Mortimer!

MORTIMER. What's the matter with you, dear?

ELAINE (*semi-hysterical*). I've almost been killed.

MORTIMER. You've almost been——(*He looks quickly at the* AUNTS.) Abby! Martha!

MARTHA. No! It was Jonathan.

ABBY. He mistook her for an sneak-thief.

ELAINE. No, it was more than that. He's some kind of maniac. Mortimer, I'm afraid of him.

MORTIMER. Why darling, you're trembling. (*Seats her on sofa. To* AUNTS.) Have you got smelling salts?

MARTHA. No, but do you think some hot tea, or coffee——?

MORTIMER. Coffee. Make some for me, too—and some sandwiches. I haven't had any dinner.

MARTHA. We'll make something for both of you.

(MORTIMER *starts to question* ELAINE *as* ABBY *takes off her hat and gloves and puts them on sideboard. Talking to* MARTHA *at the same time.*)

ABBY. Martha, we can leave our hats downstairs here, now.

(MORTIMER *turns and sees her. Steps* L.).

MORTIMER. You weren't going out somewhere, were you? Do you know what time it is? It's after twelve. (*The word twelve rings a bell.*) TWELVE! (*He turns to* ELAINE.) Elaine, you've got to go home!

ELAINE. Whaa-t?

ABBY. Why, you wanted some sandwiches for you both. It won't take a minute. (*She exits into kitchen.*)

(MORTIMER *is looking at* ELAINE *with his back to* MARTHA. MARTHA *crosses to him with shoe in hand by her* U. S. *side.*)

MARTHA. Why, don't you remember—we wanted to celebrate your engagement? (*She punctuates the word "engagement" by pointing the shoe at* MORTIMER'S *back. She looks at the shoe in wonderment. Wondering how that shoe ever got in her hand. She stares at it a moment (the other two do not see it, of course), then puts it on top of the table. Finally dismissing it she turns to* MORTIMER *again.*) That's what we'll do, dear. We'll make a nice supper for both of you (*She starts out kitchen door, then turns back.*) And we'll open a bottle of wine! (*She exits kitchen door.*)

MORTIMER (*vaguely*). All right. (*Suddenly changes his mind and runs to kitchen door.*) No WINE! (*He closes the door and comes back to* C. *as* ELAINE *rises from the sofa to him. She is still very upset.*)

ELAINE. Mortimer! What's going on in this house?

MORTIMER (*suspicious*). What do you mean—what's going on in this house?

ELAINE. You were supposed to take me to dinner and the theatre tonight you—called it off. You asked me to marry you—I said I would—and five minutes later you threw me out of the house. Tonight, just after your brother tries to strangle me, you want to chase me home. Now, listen, Mr. Brewster—before I go home, I want to know where I stand. Do you love me?

MORTIMER (*taking her hands*). I love you very much, Elaine. In fact I love you so much I can't marry you.

ELAINE. Have you suddenly gone crazy?

MORTIMER. I don't think so, but it's just a matter of time. (*They both sit on sofa as* MORTIMER *begins to explain.*) You see, insanity runs in my family. (*He looks upstairs and towards kitchen.*) It practically gallops. That's why I can't marry you, dear.

ELAINE. Now wait a minute, you've got to do better than that.

MORTIMER. No, dear—there's a strange taint in the Brewster blood. If you really knew my family it's—well—it's what you'd expect if Strindberg had written *Hellzapoppin*.

ELAINE. Now just because Teddy is a little——

MORTIMER. No, it goes way back. The first Brewster—the one who came over on the Mayflower. You know in those days the Indians used to scalp the settlers—he used to scalp the Indians.

ELAINE. Mortimer, that's ancient history.

MORTIMER. No, the whole family . . . (*He rises and points to a picture of Grandfather over the sideboard.*) Take my grandfather—he tried his patent medicines out on dead people to be sure he wouldn't kill them.

ELAINE. He wasn't so crazy. He made a million dollars.

MORTIMER. And then there's Jonathan. You just said he was a maniac—he tried to kill you.

ELAINE (*rises, crosses to him*). But he's your brother, not you. I'm in love with you.

MORTIMER. And there's Teddy, too. You *know* Teddy. He thinks he's Roosevelt. No, dear, no Brewster should marry. I realise now that if I'd met my father in time I'd have stopped him.

ELAINE. Now, darling, all this doesn't prove you're crazy. Look at your aunts—they're Brewsters, aren't they?—and the sanest, sweetest people I've ever known.

(MORTIMER *crosses above table to window-seat, speaking as he goes.*)

MORTIMER. Well, even they have their peculiarities.

ELAINE (*turning and drifting* R.). Yes, but what lovely peculiarities! —Kindness, generosity—human sympathy——

(MORTIMER *sees* ELAINE'S *back is to him. He lifts window-seat to take a peek, and sees Mr. Spenalzo instead of Mr. Hoskins. He puts window-seat down again and staggers to table, and leans on it.*)

MORTIMER (*to himself*). There's another one!

ELAINE (*turning to* MORTIMER). Oh, Mortimer, there are plenty of others. You can't tell me anything about your aunts.

MORTIMER. I'm not going to (*Crossing to her.*) Look, Elaine, you've got to go home. Something very important has just come up.

ELAINE. Up, from where? We're here alone together.

MORTIMER. I know I'm acting irrationally, but just put it down to the fact that I'm a mad Brewster.

ELAINE. If you think you're going to get out of this by pretending you're insane—you're crazy. Maybe you're not going to marry me, but I'm going to marry you. I love you, you dope!

MORTIMER (*urging her to* R. *door*). Well, if you love me will you get the hell out of here.

ELAINE. Well, at least take me home, won't you? I'm afraid.

MORTIMER. Afraid! A little walk through the cemetery?

(ELAINE *crosses to door, then changing tactics, turns to* MORTIMER.)

ELAINE. Mortimer, will you kiss me goodnight?

MORTIMER (*holding out arms*). Of course, dear. (*What* MORTIMER *plans to be a desultory peck,* ELAINE *turns into a production number. He comes out of it with no loss of poise.*) Goodnight, dear. I'll call you up in a day or two.

ELAINE (*she walks to* R. *door in a cold fury, opens it and turns to* MORTIMER). You—you critic! (*She slams door after her.*)

(MORTIMER *looks at the door helplessly then turns and stalks to the kitchen door.*)

MORTIMER (*in doorway*). Aunt Abby! Aunt Martha! come in here!

ABBY (*off stage*). We'll be in in a minute, dear.

MORTIMER. Come in here now! (*He stands down by* U. S. *end of window-seat.*)

(ABBY *enters from kitchen.*)

ABBY. Yes, dear, what is it? Where's Elaine?

MORTIMER. I thought you promised me not to let anyone in this house while I was gone!

(*The following speeches overlap.*)

ABBY. Well, Jonathan just walked in——

MORTIMER. I don't mean Jonathan——

ABBY. And Dr. Einstein was with him——

MORTIMER. I don't mean Dr. Einstein. Who's that in the window-seat?

ABBY. We told you—Mr. Hoskins.

(MORTIMER *throws open the window-seat and steps back* U. L.).

MORTIMER. It is *not* Mr. Hoskins.

(ABBY, *a little puzzled, walks to window-seat and looks in at* D. S. *end then speaks very simply.*)

ABBY. Who can that be?

MORTIMER (R. *of* ABBY). Are you trying to tell me you've never seen this man before?

ABBY. I certainly am. Why this is a fine how do you do! It's getting so anybody thinks he can walk into this house.

MORTIMER. Now Aunt Abby, don't you try to get out of this. That's another one of your gentlemen!

ABBY. Mortimer, how can you say such a thing! That man's an imposter! And if he came here to be buried in our cellar he's mistaken.

MORTIMER. Oh, Aunt Abby, you admitted to me that you put Mr. Hoskins in the window-seat.

ABBY. Yes, I did.

MORTIMER. Well, this man couldn't have just got the idea from Mr. Hoskins. By the way—where is Mr. Hoskins? (*He looks toward cellar door.*)

(ABBY *crosses above table to* U. C.)

ABBY. He must have gone to Panama.

MORTIMER. Oh, you buried him?

ABBY. No not yet. He's just down there waiting for the services, poor dear. We haven't had a minute what with Jonathan in the house. (*At the mention of* JONATHAN'S *name* MORTIMER *closes the window-seat.*) Oh, dear. We've always wanted to hold a double funeral (*crossing to kitchen door*) but I will not read services over a total stranger.

MORTIMER (*going up to her*). A stranger! Aunt Abby, how can I believe you! There are twelve men in the cellar and you admit you poisoned them.

ABBY. Yes, I did. But you don't think I'd stoop to telling a fib. Martha! (*She exits into kitchen.*)

(*At the same time* JONATHAN *enters through the arch on to balcony and comes down quickly to foot of stairs.* MORTIMER *crosses to* D. R. C. JONATHAN *sees him and crosses to him.*)

JONATHAN. Oh, Mortimer—I'd like to have a word with you.

MORTIMER (*standing up to him*). A word's about all you'll have time for, Jonathan, because I've decided you and your Doctor friend are going to have to get out of this house just as quickly as possible.

JONATHAN (*smoothly*). I'm glad you recognise the fact that you and I can't live under the same roof—but you've arrived at the wrong solution. Take your suitcase and get out! (*He starts to cross above* MORTIMER, *anxious to get to the window-seat, but* MORTIMER *makes big sweep around above table and comes back to him at* D. S. C.).

MORTIMER. Jonathan!—You're beginning to bore me. You've played your one night stand in Brooklyn—move on!

JONATHAN. My dear Mortimer, just because you've graduated from the back fence to the typewriter, don't think you've grown up . . .(*He takes a sudden step* U. S. *around* MORTIMER *and gets to the window-seat and sits*). I'm staying, and you're leaving—and I mean now!

MORTIMER (*crossing to him*). If you think I can be frightened—if you think there's anything I fear——

JONATHAN (*he rises, they stand facing each other*). I've lived a strange life, Mortimer. But it's taught me one thing—to be afraid of nothing! (*They glare at each other with equal courage when* ABBY *marches in from kitchen, followed by* MARTHA.)

ABBY. Martha, just look and see what's in that window-seat.

(*Both* MEN *throw themselves on the window-seat simultaneously.* JONATHAN D. S. *end.*)

MORTIMER AND JONATHAN. Now, Aunt Abby!

(MORTIMER *turns his head slowly to* JONATHAN, *light dawning on his face. He rises with smiling assurance.*)

MORTIMER. Jonathan, let Aunt Martha see what's in the window-seat. (JONATHAN *freezes dangerously,* MORTIMER *crosses below table up to* ABBY.) Aunt Abby, I owe you an apology. (*He kisses her on forehead.*) I have very good news for you. Jonathan is leaving. He's taking Dr. Einstein and their cold companion with him. (JONATHAN *rises but holds his ground.*) Jonathan, you're my brother. You're a Brewster. I'm going to give you a chance to get away and take the evidence with you—you can't ask for more than that. (JONATHAN *doesn't move.*) Very well,—in that case I'll have to call the police. (MORTIMER *crosses to phone and picks it up.*)

JONATHAN. Don't reach for that telephone. (*He crosses to* L. *of* MORTIMER.) Are you still giving me orders after seeing what's happened to Mr. Spenalzo.

MARTHA (*she's above table*). Spenalzo?

ABBY (U. C.). I knew he was a foreigner.

JONATHAN. Remember what happened to Mr. Spenalzo can happen to you too.

(*There is a knock on* R. *door.* ABBY *crosses and opens it and* OFFICER O'HARA *sticks his head in.*)

O'HARA. Hello, Miss Abby.

ABBY. Oh, Officer O'Hara. Is there something we can do for you?

(MORTIMER *puts phone down and drifts down close to* O'HARA. JONATHAN *turns* L.).

O'HARA. I saw your lights on and thought there might be sickness in the house. (*He sees* MORTIMER.) Oh, you got company—I'm sorry I disturbed you.

MORTIMER (*taking* O'HARA *by the arm*). No, no, come in.

ABBY. Yes, come in.

MARTHA (*crossing to door*). Come right in, Officer O'Hara. (MORTIMER *leads* O'HARA *in a couple of steps and shuts door.* ABBY *crosses back to* U. S. C. MARTHA *is near desk.* JONATHAN *is in front of sofa* R. *of* ABBY. MARTHA, *to* O'HARA.) This is our nephew, Mortimer.

O'HARA. Pleased to meet you.

(JONATHAN *starts toward kitchen.*)

ABBY (*stopping* JONATHAN). And this is another nephew, Jonathan.

O'HARA (*crosses below* MORTIMER *and gestures to* JONATHAN *with his night stick*). Pleased to make your acquaintance. (JONATHAN *ignores him.* O'HARA *speaks to* AUNTS.) Well, it must be nice havin' your nephews visitin' you. Are they going to stay with you for a bit?

MORTIMER. I'm staying. My brother Jonathan is just leaving.

(JONATHAN *starts for stairs.* O'HARA *stops him.*)

O'HARA. I've met you here before, haven't I?

ABBY. I'm afraid not. Jonathan hasn't been home for years.

O'HARA. Your face looks familiar to me. Maybe I seen a picture of you somewheres.

JONATHAN. I don't think so. (*He hurries upstairs.*)

MORTIMER. Yes, Jonathan, I'd hurry if I were you. Your things are all packed anyway, aren't they?

O'HARA. Well, you'll be wanting to say your goodbyes. I'll be running along.

MORTIMER. What's the rush? I'd like to have you stick around until my brother goes.

(JONATHAN *exits through arch.*)

O'HARA. I just dropped in to make sure everything was all right.

MORTIMER. We're going to have some coffee in a minute. Won't you join us?

ABBY. Oh, I forgot the coffee. (*She goes out to kitchen.*)

MARTHA (*crossing to kitchen door*). Well, I'd better make some more sandwiches. I ought to know your appetite by this time, Officer O'Hara. (*She goes out to kitchen as* O'HARA *follows as far as* C.).

O'HARA. Don't bother. I'm due to ring in in a few minutes.

MORTIMER. You can have a cup of coffee with us. My brother will be gone soon. (*She leads* O'HARA *below table to armchair.*) Sit down.

O'HARA. Say—ain't I seen a photograph of your brother around here some place?

MORTIMER. I don't think so. (*He sits* R. *of table.*)

O'HARA. He certainly reminds me of somebody.

MORTIMER. He looks like somebody you've probably seen in the movies.

O'HARA. I never go to the movies. I hate' em! My mother says the movies is a bastard art.

MORTIMER. Yes, it's full of them. Your, er, mother said that?

O'HARA. Yeah, My mother was an actress—a stage actress. Perhaps you heard of her—Peaches Latour.

MORTIMER. It sounds like a name I've seen on a programme. What did she play?

O'HARA. Well, her big hit was "Mutt and Jeff." Played it for three years. I was born on tour—the third season.

MORTIMER. You were?

O'HARA. Yep. Sioux City, Iowa. I was born in the dressing-room at the end of the second act, and Mother made the finale.

MORTIMER. What a trouper! There must be a good story in your mother—you know, I write about the theatre.

O'HARA. You do? Saay!—you're not Mortimer Brewster, the dramatic critic!

MORTIMER. Yes.

O'HARA. Well, I certainly am glad to meet you. (*He moves his hat and stick preparatory to shaking hand with* MORTIMER. *He also picks up the sport shoe which* MARTHA *has left on the table. He looks at it just for a split second and puts it on the* D. S. *end of table.* MORTIMER *sees it and stares at it.*) Say, Mr. Brewster—we're in the same line of business.

MORTIMER (*still intent on shoe.*) We are?

O'HARA. Yeah. I'm a playwright. Oh, this being on the police force is just temporary.

MORTIMER. How long have you been on the force?

O'HARA. Twelve years. I'm collecting material for a play.

MORTIMER. I'll bet it's a honey.

O'HARA. Well, it ought to be. With all the drama I see being a cop. Mr. Brewster—you got no idea what goes on in Brooklyn.

MORTIMER. I think I have. (*He puts the shoe under his chair then looks at his watch, than looks towards balcony.*)

O'HARA. Say, what time you got?

MORTIMER. Ten after one.

O'HARA. Gee, I gotta ring in. (*He starts for* R. *door but* MORTIMER *stops him at* C.).

MORTIMER. Wait a minute. O'Hara. On that play of yours—I may be able to help you. (*Sits him in chair* R.).

O'HARA (*ecstasy*). You would! (*Rises.*) Say, it was fate my walking in here tonight. Look—I'll tell you the plot!

(*At this point* JONATHAN *enters on the balcony followed by* DR. EINSTEIN. *They each have a bag. At the same moment* ABBY *enters from kitchen. Helpful as the cop has been,* MORTIMER *does not want to listen to his plot. As he backs away from him he speaks to* JONATHAN *as they come downstairs.*)

MORTIMER. Oh, you're on your way, eh? Good! You haven't got much time, you know.

ABBY (U. L.). Well, everything's just about ready. (*Sees* JONATHAN *and* EINSTEIN *at foot of stairs.*) Oh, you leaving now. Jonathan? Goodbye, Dr. Einstein. (*She sees instrument case above window-seat*). Oh, doesn't this case belong to you?

(*This reminds* MORTIMER *of Mr. Spenalzo, also.*)

MORTIMER. Yes, Jonathan—you can't go without all of your things. (*Now to get rid of* O'HARA. *He turns to him.*) Well, O'Hara, it was nice meeting you. I'll see you again and we'll talk about your play.

O'HARA (*refusing to leave*). Oh, I'm not leaving now, Mr. Brewster.

MORTIMER. Why not?

O'HARA. Well, you just offered to help me with my play, didn't you? You and me are going to write my play together.

MORTIMER. I can't do that O'Hara—I'm not a creative writer.

O'HARA. I'll do the creating. You just put the words to it.

MORTIMER. But, O'Hara——

O'HARA. No, sir, Mr. Brewster. I ain't leaving this window till I tell you the plot. (*He crosses and sits on the window-seat.*)

JONATHAN (*starting for* R. *door.*) In that case, Mortimer ... we'll be running along.

MORTIMER. Don't try that. You can't go yet. You've got to take *everything* with you, you know. (*He turns and sees* O'HARA *on window-seat and runs to him.*) Look, O'Hara, you run along now, eh? My brother's just going——

O'HARA. I can wait. I've been waiting twelve years.

(MARTHA *enters from kitchen with a tray of coffee and sandwiches.*)

MARTHA. I'm sorry I was so long.

MORTIMER. Don't bring that in here. O'Hara, would you join us for a bit in the kitchen?

MARTHA. The kitchen?

ABBY (*to* MARTHA). Jonathan's leaving.

MARTHA. Oh. Well, that's nice. Come along, Officer O'Hara. (*She exits to kitchen.*)

(O'HARA *gets to kitchen doorway as* ABBY *speaks.*)

ABBY. Sure you don't mind eating in the kitchen, Mr. O'Hara?

O'HARA. And where else would you eat?

ABBY. Goodbye, Jonathan, nice to have seen you again.

(O'HARA *exits to kitchen, followed by* ABBY. MORTIMER *crosses to kitchen doorway and shuts door, then turns to* JONATHAN.)

MORTIMER. I'm glad you came back to Brooklyn, Jonathan, because it gives me a chance to throw you out—and the first one out is your boy friend, Mr. Spenalzo.

(*He lifts up window-seat. As he does so,* O'HARA, *sandwich in hand, enters from kitchen.* MORTIMER *drops window-seat.*)

O'HARA. Look, Mr. Brewster, we can talk in here.

MORTIMER (*pushing him into kitchen*). Coming right out.

JONATHAN. I might have known you'd grow up to write a play with a policeman.

MORTIMER (*from kitchen doorway*). Get going now—all three of you. (*He exits, shutting door.*)

(JONATHAN *puts bag down and crosses to window-seat.*)

JONATHAN. Doctor, this affair between my brother and me has got to be settled.

EINSTEIN (*crossing to window-seat for instrument case and bringing it back to foot of stairs*). Now, Chonny, we got trouble enough. Your brother gives us a chance to get away—what more could you ask?

JONATHAN. You don't understand. (*He lifts window-seat.*) This goes back a good many years.

EINSTEIN (*foot of stairs*). Now, Chonny, let's get going.

JONATHAN (*harshly*). We're not going. We're going to sleep right here tonight.

EINSTEIN. With a cop in the kitchen and Mr Spenalzo in the window-seat.

JONATHAN. That's all he's got on us. (*Puts window-seat down.*) We'll take Mr. Spenalzo down and dump him in the bay, and come right back here.—Then if he tries to interfere——(*He crosses to* C. EINSTEIN *crosses to* L. *of him and faces him.*)

EINSTEIN. Now, Chonny.

JONATHAN. Doctor, you know when I make up my mind——

EINSTEIN. Yeah—when you make up your mind, you lose your head. Brooklyn ain't a good place for you.

JONATHAN (*peremptorily*). Doctor!

EINSTEIN. O.K. We got to stick together. (*He crosses to bags.*) Some day we get stuck together. If we're coming back here do we got to take these with us?

JONATHAN. No. Leave them here. Hide them in the cellar. Move fast! (*He moves to bags to* L. *end of sofa as* EINSTEIN *goes down cellar with instrument case.*) Spenalzo can go out the same way he came in! (*He kneels on window-seat and looks out. Then as he starts to lift window-seat,* EINSTEIN *comes in from the cellar with some excitement.*)

EINSTEIN. Hey, Chonny, come quick!

JONATHAN (*crossing to him.*). What's the matter?

EINSTEIN. You know that hole in the cellar?

JONATHAN. Yes.

EINSTEIN. We got an *ace* in the hole. Come on I show you. (*They both exit into cellar,* JONATHAN *shuts door.*)

(MORTIMER *enters from kitchen, sees their bags still there. He opens window-seat and sees Spenalzo. Then he puts his head out window and yells.*)

MORTIMER. Jonathan! Jonathan! (JONATHAN *comes through cellar door unnoticed by* MORTIMER *and crosses to back of him.* EINSTEIN *comes down into* C. *of room.*) Jonathan!

JONATHAN (*quietly*). Yes, Mortimer.

MORTIMER (*leaping backwards to below table.*) Where have you two been? I thought I told you to get—

JONATHAN. We're not going.

MORTIMER. Oh, you're not? You think I'm not serious about this, eh? Do you want O'Hara to know what's in that window-seat?

JONATHAN. We're staying here.

MORTIMER (*crossing around table to kitchen door*). All right! You asked for it. This gets me rid of you and Officer O'Hara at the same time. (*Opens kitchen door, yells out.*) Officer O'Hara, come in here!

JONATHAN. If you tell O'Hara what's in the window-seat, I'll tell him what's down in the cellar.

(MORTIMER *closes kitchen door quickly.*)

MORTIMER. The cellar?

JONATHAN. There's an elderly gentleman down there who seems to be very dead.

MORTIMER. What were you doing down in the cellar?

EINSTEIN. What's *he* doing down in the cellar?

(O'HARA's *voice is heard off stage.*)

O'HARA. No, thanks, ma'am. They were fine. I've plenty.

JONATHAN. Now what are you going to say to O'Hara?

(O'HARA *walks in kitchen door.*)

O'HARA. Say, Mr. Brewster, your aunts want to hear it too. Shall I get them in here?

MORTIMER (*pulling him* R.). No. O'Hara, you can't do that now. You've got to ring in.

(O'HARA *stops at* C. *as* MORTIMER *opens door.*)

O'HARA. The hell with ringing in. I'll get your aunts in here and tell you the plot. (*He starts for kitchen door.*)

MORTIMER (*grabbing him*). No, O'Hara, not in front of all these people. We'll get together alone, some place later.

O'HARA. How about the back room at Kelly's?

MORTIMER (*passing* O'HARA R. *in front of him*). Fine! You go ring in, and I'll meet you at Kelly's.

JONATHAN (*at window-seat*). Why don't you two go down in the cellar?

O'HARA. That's all right with me. (*Starts for cellar door.*) Is this the cellar?

MORTIMER (*grabbing him again, pushing toward door*). Nooo! We'll go to Kelly's. But you're going to ring in on the way.

O'HARA (*as he exits* R.). All right, that'll only take a couple of minutes. (*He's gone.*)

(MORTIMER *takes his hat from hall tree and crosses to open* R. *door.*)

MORTIMER. I'll ditch this guy and be back in five minutes. I'll expect to find you gone. (*Changes his mind.*) Wait for me, (*He exits* R.).

(EINSTEIN *sits* R. *of table.*)

JONATHAN. We'll wait for him, Doctor. I've waited a great many years for a chance like this.

EINSTEIN. We got him right where we want him. Did he look guilty!

JONATHAN (*rising*). Take the bags up to our room, Doctor.

(EINSTEIN *gets bags and reaches foot of stairs with them.* ABBY *and* MARTHA *enter from kitchen.* ABBY *speaks as she enters.*)

ABBY. Have they gone? (*Sees* JONATHAN *and* EINSTEIN.) Oh——we thought we heard somebody leave.

JONATHAN (*crossing to* R.C.). Just Mortimer, and he'll be back in a few minutes. Is there any food left in the kitchen? I think Dr. Einstein and I would enjoy a bite.

MARTHA (L. *of table*). But you won't have time.

ABBY (*at* C.). No, if you're still here when Mortimer gets back he won't like it.

EINSTEIN (*dropping* D. S. R.). He'll like it. He's gotta like it.

JONATHAN. Get something for us to eat while we bury Mr. Spenalzo in the cellar.

MARTHA (*crossing to below table*). Oh no!

ABBY. He can't stay in our cellar. No, Jonathan, you've got to take him with you.

JONATHAN. There's a friend of Mortimer's downstairs waiting for him.

ABBY. A friend of Mortimer's?

JONATHAN. He and Mr. Spenalzo will get along fine together. They're both dead.

MARTHA. They must mean Mr. Hoskins.

EINSTEIN. Mr. Hoskins?

JONATHAN. You know about what's downstairs?

ABBY. Of course we do, and he's no friend of Mortimer's. He's one of our gentlemen.

EINSTEIN. Your chentlemen?

MARTHA. And we won't have any strangers buried in our cellar.

JONATHAN (*uncomprehending*). But Mr. Hoskins——

MARTHA. Mr. Hoskins isn't a stranger.

ABBY. Besides, there's no room for Mr. Spenalzo. The cellar's crowded already.

JONATHAN. Crowded? With what?

ABBY. There are twelve graves down there now.

(*The two* MEN *back in amazement.*)

JONATHAN. Twelve graves!

ABBY. That leaves very little room and we're going to need it.

JONATHAN. You mean you and Aunt Martha have murdered——?

ABBY. Murdered! Certainly not. It's one of our charities.

MARTHA (*indignantly*). Why, what we've been doing is a mercy.

ABBY (*gesturing outside*). So you just take your Mr. Spenalzo out of here.

JONATHAN (*still unable to believe*). You've done that—here in this house—(*points to floor*) and you've buried them down there!

EINSTEIN. Chonny—we've been chased all over the world—they stay right here in Brooklyn and do just as good as you do.

JONATHAN (*facing him*). What?

EINSTEIN. You've got twelve and they've got twelve.

JONATHAN (*slowly*). I've got thirteen.

EINSTEIN. No, Chonny, twelve.

JONATHAN. Thirteen! (*Counting on fingers*). There's Mr. Spenalzo. Then the first one in London—two in Johannesburg—one in Sydney—one in Melbourne—two in San Francisco—two in Phoenix, Arizona——

EINSTEIN. Phoenix?

JONATHAN. The filling station. The three in Chicago and the one in South Bend. That makes thirteen!

EINSTEIN. But you can't count the one in South Bend. He died of pneumonia.

JONATHAN. He wouldn't have got pneumonia if I hadn't shot him.

EINSTEIN (*adamant*). No, Chonny, he died of pneumonia. He don't count.

JONATHAN. He counts with me. I say thirteen.

EINSTEIN. No, Chonny, You got twelve and they got twelve. (*Crossing to* Aunts.) The old ladies are just as good as you are.

(*The two* AUNTS *smile at each other happily.* JONATHAN *turns, facing the three of them and speaks menacingly.*)

JONATHAN. Oh, they are, are they? Well, that's easily taken care of. All I need is one more, that's all—just one more.

(MORTIMER *enters hastily* R., *closing door behind him, and turns to them with a nervous smile.*)

MORTIMER. Well, here I am!

(JONATHAN *turns and looks at him with the widening eyes of someone who has just solved a problem, as the curtain falls.*)

ACT THREE

Scene One

The scene is the same. Still later that night.

The curtain rises on an empty stage. The window-seat is open and we see that it's empty. The armchair has been shifted to R. of table. The curtains over the windows are closed. All doors except cellar are closed. ABBY's hymnal and black gloves are on table. MARTHA's hymnal and gloves are on sideboard. Otherwise the room is the same. As the curtain rises we hear a row from the cellar, through the open door. The speeches overlap in excitement and anger until the AUNTS appear on the stage, from cellar door.

MARTHA. You stop doing that!

ABBY. This is our house and this is our cellar and you can't do that.

EINSTEIN. Ladies! Please!—Go back upstairs where you belong.

JONATHAN. Abby! Martha! Go upstairs!

MARTHA. There's no use your doing what you're doing because it will just have to be undone.

ABBY. I tell you we won't have it and you'd better stop it right now.

MARTHA (*entering from cellar*). All right! You'll find out. You'll find out whose house this is. (*She crosses to door* D. R., *opens it and looks out. Then closes it.*)

ABBY (*entering*). I'm warning you! You'd better stop it! (D. S. C. *To* MARTHA.) Hasn't Mortimer come back yet?

MARTHA. No.

ABBY. It's a terrible thing to do—to bury a good Methodist with a foreigner. (*She crosses to window-seat.*)

MARTHA (*crossing to cellar door*). I will not have our cellar desecrated!

ABBY (*drops window-seat*). And we promised Mr. Hoskins a full Christian funeral. Where do you suppose Mortimer went?

MARTHA (*drops* D. S.). I don't know, but he must be doing something—because he said to Jonathan, "You just wait, I'll settle this."

ABBY (*crossing up to sideboard*). Well, he can't very well settle it while he's out of the house. That's all we want settled—what's going on down there.

(MORTIMER *enters* R., *closes door.*)

MORTIMER (*as one who has everything settled*). All right. Now, where's Teddy?

(*The* AUNTS *are very much annoyed with* MORTIMER.)

ABBY. Mortimer, where have you been?

MORTIMER. I've been over to Dr. Gilchrist's. I've got his signature on Teddy's commitment papers.

MARTHA. Mortimer, what is the matter with you?

ABBY (*to below table*). Running around getting papers signed at a time like this!

MARTHA. Do you know what Jonathan's doing?

ABBY. He's putting Mr. Hoskins and Mr. Spenalzo in together.

MORTIMER. (*to cellar door*). Oh, he is, is he? Well, let him. (*He shuts cellar door.*) Is Teddy in his room?

MARTHA. Teddy won't be any help.

MORTIMER. When he signs these commitment papers I can tackle Jonathan.

ABBY. What have they got to do with it?

MORTIMER. You had to go and tell Jonathan about those twelve graves. If I can make Teddy responsible for those I can protect you, don't you see?

ABBY. No, I don't see. And we pay taxes to have the police protect us.

MORTIMER (*going upstairs*). I'll be back down in a minute.

ABBY (*takes gloves and hymnal from table*). Come Martha. We're going for the police.

(MARTHA *gets her gloves and hymnal from sideboard. They both start* R. *to door.*)

MORTIMER (*on landing*). All right. (*He turns and rushes downstairs to* R. *door before they can reach it.*) The police. You can't go for the police.

LIVERPOOL JOHN MOORES UNIVERSITY
LEARNING SERVICES

MARTHA (D. R., *but* L. *of* ABBY). Why can't we?

MORTIMER (*near* R. *door*). Because if you tell the police about Mr. Spenalzo they'd find Mr. Hoskins too (*crosses to* MARTHA), and that might make them curious, and they'd find out about the other twelve gentlemen.

ABBY. Mortimer, we know the police better than you do. I don't think they'd pry into our private affairs if we asked them not to.

MORTIMER. But if they found your twelve gentlemen they'd have to report to headquarters.

MARTHA (*pulling on her gloves*). I'm not so sure they'd bother. They'd have to make out a very long report—and if there's one thing a policeman hates to do, it's to write.

MORTIMER. You can't depend on that. It might leak out!—and you couldn't expect a judge and jury to understand.

MARTHA. Oh, Judge Cullman would.

ABBY (*drawing on her gloves*). We know him very well.

MARTHA. He always comes to church to pray—just before election.

ABBY. And he's coming here to tea some day. He promised.

MARTHA. Oh, Abby, we must speak to him again about that. (*To* MORTIMER.) His wife died a few years ago and it's left him very lonely.

ABBY. Well, come along, Martha. (*She starts toward door* R. MORTIMER *gets there first.*)

MORTIMER. No! You can't do this. I won't let you. You can't leave this house, and you can't have Judge Cullman to tea.

ABBY. Well, if you're not going to do something about Mr. Spenalzo, we are.

MORTIMER. I am going to do something. We may have to call the police in later, but if we do, I want to be ready for them.

MARTHA. You've got to get Jonathan out of this house!

ABBY. And Mr. Spenalzo, too!

MORTIMER. Will you please let me do this my own way? (*He starts upstairs*). I've got to see Teddy.

ABBY (*facing* MORTIMER *on stairs*). If they're not out of here by morning, Mortimer, we're going to call the police.

MORTIMER. (*on balcony*). They'll be out, I promise you that! Go to bed, will you? And for God's sake get out of those clothes—you look like Judith Anderson. (*He exits into hall, closing door.*)

(*The two* AUNTS *watch him off.* MARTHA *turns to* ABBY.)

MARTHA. Well, Abby, that's a relief, isn't it?

ABBY. Yes—if Mortimer's really going to do something at last, it just means Jonathan's going to a lot of unnecessary trouble. We'd better tell him. (ABBY *starts to cellar door as* JONATHAN *comes in. They meet* U. S. C. *front of sofa. His clothes are dirty.*) Oh, Jonathan—you might as well stop what you're doing.

JONATHAN. It's all done. Did I hear Mortimer?

ABBY. Well, it will just have to be undone. You're all going to be out of this house by morning. Mortimer's promised.

JONATHAN. Oh, are we? In that case, you and Aunt Martha can go to bed and have a pleasant night's sleep.

MARTHA (*always a little frightened by* JONATHAN, *starts upstairs*). Yes. Come, Abby.

(ABBY *follows* MARTHA *upstairs.*)

JONATHAN. Goodnight, Aunties.

ABBY. Not goodnight, Jonathan. Goodbye. By the time we get up you'll be out of this house. Mortimer's promised.

MARTHA (*on balcony*). And he has a way of doing it too!

JONATHAN. Then Mortimer is back?

ABBY. Oh, yes, he's up here talking to Teddy.

MARTHA. Goodbye, Jonathan.

ABBY. Goodbye, Jonathan.

JONATHAN. Perhaps you'd better say goodbye to Mortimer.

ABBY. Oh, you'll see Mortimer.

JONATHAN (*sitting on stool*). Yes—I'll see Mortimer.

(ABBY *and* MARTHA *exit.* JONATHAN *sits without moving. There is murder in his thought.* EINSTEIN *enters from the cellar. He dusts off his trouser cuffs, lifting his leg, and we see he is wearing Spenalzo's sport shoes.*)

EINSTEIN. Whew! That's all fixed up. Smooth like a lake. Nobody'd ever know they were down there. (JONATHAN *still sits without moving.*) That bed feels good already. Forty-eight hours we didn't sleep. (*Crossing to second stair.*) Come on, Chonny, let's go up, yes?

JONATHAN. You're forgetting, Doctor.

EINSTEIN. Vat?

JONATHAN. My brother Mortimer.

EINSTEIN. Chonny—tonight? We do that tomorrow or the next day.

JONATHAN (*just able to control himself*). No, tonight! Now!

EINSTEIN (*down to floor*). Chonny, please—I'm tired—and tomorrow I got to operate.

JONATHAN. Yes, you're operating tomorrow, Doctor. But tonight we take care of Mortimer.

EINSTEIN (*kneeling in front of* JONATHAN, *trying to pacify him*). But, Chonny, not tonight—we go to bed, eh?

JONATHAN (*rising.* EINSTEIN *straightens up too*). Doctor, look at me. You can see it's going to be done, can't you?

EINSTEIN (*retreating*). Ach, Chonny—I can see. I know dat look!

JONATHAN. It's a little too late for us to dissolve our partnership.

EINSTEIN. O.K., we do it. But the quick way. The quick twist like in London. (*He gives that London neck another twist with his hands and makes a noise suggesting strangulation.*)

JONATHAN. No, Doctor, I think this calls for something special. (*He walks towards* EINSTEIN, *who breaks* U. S. JONATHAN *has the look of beginning to anticipate a rare pleasure.*) I think perhaps the Melbourne method.

EINSTEIN. Chonny—no—not that. Two hours! And when it was all over, what? The fellow in London was just as dead as the fellow in Melbourne.

JONATHAN. We had to work too fast in London. There was no aesthetic satisfaction in it—but Melbourne, ah, there was something to remember.

EINSTEIN (*dropping* D. S. *as* JONATHAN *crosses him*). Remember! (*He shivers.*) I vish I didn't. No, Chonny—not Melbourne—not me!

JONATHAN. Yes, Doctor. Where are the instruments?

EINSTEIN. I won't do it, Chonny. I won't do it.

JONATHAN (*advancing on him as* EINSTEIN *backs* D. S.). Get your instruments!

EINSTEIN. No, Chonny!

JONATHAN. Where are they? Oh, yes—you hid them in the cellar. Where?

EINSTEIN. I won't tell you.

JONATHAN (*going to cellar door*). I'll find them, Doctor. (*He exits to cellar, closing door.*)

(TEDDY *enters on balcony and lifts his bugle to blow.* MORTIMER *dashes out and grabs his arm.* EINSTEIN *has rushed to cellar door. He stands there as* MORTIMER *and* TEDDY *speak.*)

MORTIMER. Don't do that, Mr. President.

TEDDY. I cannot sign any proclamation without consulting my cabinet.

MORTIMER. But this must be a secret.

TEDDY. A secret proclamation? How unusual.

MORTIMER. Japan mustn't know until it's signed.

TEDDY. Japan! Those yellow devils. I'll sign it right away. (*Taking legal paper from* MORTIMER.) You have my word for it. I can let the cabinet know later.

MORTIMER. Yes, let's go and sign it.

TEDDY. You wait here. A secret proclamation has to be signed in secret.

MORTIMER. But at once, Mr. President.

TEDDY. I'll have to put on my signing clothes. (TEDDY *exits.*)

(MORTIMER *comes downstairs.* EINSTEIN *crosses and takes Mortimer's hat off of hall tree and hands it to him.*)

EINSTEIN (*anxious to get* MORTIMER *out of the house*). Ah, you go now, eh?

MORTIMER (*takes hat and puts it on desk*). No, Doctor, I'm waiting for something. Something important.

EINSTEIN (L. *of* MORTIMER). Please—you go now!

MORTIMER. Dr. Einstein, I have nothing against you personally. You seem to be a nice fellow. Take my advice and get out of this house and get just as far away as possible.

EINSTEIN. Trouble, yah! You get out.

MORTIMER (*crossing to* C.). All right, don't say I didn't warn you.

EINSTEIN. I'm warning you—get away quick.

MORTIMER. Things are going to start popping around here any minute.

EINSTEIN (D. R.). Listen—Chonny's in a bad mood. When he's like dis, he's a madman—things happen—terrible things.

MORTIMER. Jonathan doesn't worry me now.

EINSTEIN. Ach, himmel—don't those plays you see teach you anything?

MORTIMER. About what?

EINSTEIN. Vell, at least people in plays act like they got sense—that's more than you do.

MORTIMER (*interested in this observation*). Oh, you think so, do you? You think people in plays act intelligently. I wish you had to sit through some of the ones I have to sit through. Take the little opus I saw tonight for instance. In this play, there's a man—he's supposed to be bright . . . (JONATHAN *enters from cellar with instrument case, stands in doorway and listens to* MORTIMER)—he knows he's in a house with murderers—he ought to know he's in danger—he's even been warned to get out of the house—but does he go? No, he stays there. Now I ask you, Doctor, is that what an intelligent person would do?

EINSTEIN. You're asking me?

MORTIMER. He didn't even have sense enough to be frightened, to be on guard. For instance, the murderer invites him to sit down.

EINSTEIN (*he moves so as to keep* MORTIMER *from seeing* JONATHAN). You mean—"Won't you sit down?"

MORTIMER (*reaches out and pulls armchair to him* R. *of table without turning his head from* EINSTEIN). Believe it or not, that one was in there too.

EINSTEIN. And what did he do?

MORTIMER (*sitting in armchair*). He sat down. Now mind you, this fellow's supposed to be bright. There he sits—just waiting to be trussed up. And what do you think they use to tie him with?

EINSTEIN. Vat?

MORTIMER. The curtain cord.

(JONATHAN *spies curtain cords on either side of window in* L. *wall. He crosses, stands on window-seat and cuts cords with penknife.*)

EINSTEIN. Vell, why not? A good idea. Very convenient.

MORTIMER. A little too convenient. When are playwrights going to use some imagination! The curtain cord!

(JONATHAN *has got the curtain cord and is moving in slowly behind* MORTIMER).

EINSTEIN. He didn't see him get it?

MORTIMER. See him? He sat there with his back to him. That's the kind of stuff we have to suffer through night after night. And they say the critics are killing the theatre—it's the playwrights who are killing the theatre. So there he sits—the big dope—this fellow who's supposed to be bright—just waiting to be trussed up and gagged.

(JONATHAN *drops loop of curtain cord over* MORTIMER'S *shoulder and draws it taut. At the same time he throws other loop of cord on floor beside* EINSTEIN. *Simultaneously,* EINSTEIN *leaps to* MORTIMER *and gags him with handkerchief, then takes his curtain cord and ties* MORTIMER'S *legs to chair.*)

EINSTEIN. (*finishing up the tying*). You're right about dat fella—he vasn't very bright.

JONATHAN. Now, Mortimer, if you don't mind—we'll finish the story. (*He goes to sideboard and brings two candelabra to table and speaks as he lights them.* EINSTEIN *remains kneeling beside* MORTIMER.) Mortimer, I've been away for twenty years, but never once in all that time—my dear brother—were you out of my mind. In Melbourne one night, I dreamed of you—when I landed in San Francisco I felt a strange satisfaction—once more I was in the same country with you. (JONATHAN *has finished lighting candles. He crosses* D. R. *and flips light-switch, darkening stage. As he crosses,* EINSTEIN *gets up and crosses to window-seat.* JONATHAN *picks up instrument case at cellar doorway and sets it on table between candelabra and opens it, revealing various surgical instruments both in the bottom of case and on the inside of the cover.*) Now, Doctor, we go to work! (*He removes an instrument from the case and fingers it lovingly, as* EINSTEIN *crosses and kneels on chair* L. *of table. He is not too happy about all this.*)

EINSTEIN. Please, Chonny, for me, the quick way!

JONATHAN. Doctor! This must really be an artistic achievement. After all, we're performing before a very distinguished critic.

EINSTEIN. Chonny!

JONATHAN (*flaring*). Doctor!

EINSTEIN (*beaten*). All right. Let's get it over. (*He closes curtains tightly and sits on window-seat.* JONATHAN *takes three or four more instruments out of the case and fingers them. At last, having the necessary equipment laid out on the towel* [*all in case*] *he begins to put on a pair of rubber gloves* [*also in case*].)

JONATHAN. All ready for you, Doctor!

EINSTEIN. I gotta have a drink. I can't do this without a drink. (*He takes bottle from pocket. Drinks. Finds it's empty. Rises.*)

JONATHAN. Pull yourself together, Doctor.

EINSTEIN. I gotta have a drink. Ven ve valked in here this afternoon there was wine here—remember? Vere did she put that? (*He looks at sideboard and remembers. He goes to it, opens* L. *cupboard and brings bottle and two wine glasses to* D. S. *end of table top.*) Look, Chonny, we got a drink. (*He pours wine into the two glasses, emptying the bottle.* MORTIMER *watches him.*) Dat's all dere is. I split it with you. We both need a drink. (*He hands one glass to* JONATHAN, *then raises his own glass to his lips.* JONATHAN *stops him.*)

JONATHAN. One moment, Doctor—please. Where are your manners? (*He drops* D. S. *to* R. *of* MORTIMER *and looks at him.*) Yes, Mortimer, I realise now it was you who brought me back to Brooklyn . . . (*He looks at wine, then draws it back and forth under his nose smelling it. He decides that it's all right apparently for he raises his glass—*) Doctor—to my dear dead brother——

(*As they get the glasses to their lips,* TEDDY *steps out on the balcony and blows a terrific call on his bugle.* EINSTEIN *and* JONATHAN *drop their glasses, spilling the wine.* TEDDY *turns and exits.*)

EINSTEIN. Ach, Gott!

JONATHAN. Damn that idiot! (*He starts for stairs.* EINSTEIN *rushes over and intercepts him.*) He goes next! That's all—he goes next!

EINSTEIN. No, Chonny, not Teddy—that's where I shtop—not Teddy!

JONATHAN. We get to Teddy later!

EINSTEIN. We don't get to him at all.

JONATHAN. Now we've got to work fast! (*He crosses above to* L. *of* MORTIMER. EINSTEIN *in front of* MORTIMER.)

EINSTEIN. Yah, the quick way—eh Chonny?

JONATHAN. Yes, Doctor, the quick way! (*He pulls a large silk handkerchief from his inside pocket and drops it around* MORTIMER'S *neck.*)

(*At this point the door bursts open and* OFFICER O'HARA *comes to* C., *very excited.*)

O'HARA. Hey! The Colonel's gotta quit blowing that horn!

JONATHAN (*he and* EINSTEIN *are standing in front of* MORTIMER, *hiding him from* O'HARA). It's all right, Officer. We're taking the bugle away from him.

O'HARA. There's going to be hell to pay in the morning. We promised the neighbours he wouldn't do that any more.

JONATHAN. It won't happen again, Officer. Goodnight.

O'HARA. I'd better speak to him myself. Where are the lights? (O'HARA *puts on lights and goes upstairs to landing, when he sees* MORTIMER). Hey! You stood me up. I waited an hour at Kelly's for you. (*He comes downstairs and over to* MORTIMER *and looks at him then speaks to* JONATHAN *and* EINSTEIN.) What happened to him?

EINSTEIN (*thinking fast*). He was explaining the play he saw tonight—that's what happened to the fella in the play.

O'HARA. Did they have that in the play you saw tonight? (MORTIMER *nods his head—yes.*) Gee, they practically stole that

from the second act on my play—— (*He starts to explain.*) Why,
in my second act, just before the—— (*He turns back to*
MORTIMER.) I'd better begin at the beginning. It opens in my
mother's dressing room, where I was born—only I ain't born
yet—— (MORTIMER *rubs his shoes together to attract* O'HARA'S
attention.) Huh? Oh, yeah. (O'HARA *starts to remove the gag from*
MORTIMER'S *mouth and then decides not to.*) No! You've got to hear
the plot. (*He gets stool and brings it to* R. *of* MORTIMER *and sits,
continuing on with his "plot" as the curtain falls.*) Well, she's sitting
there making up, see—when all of a sudden through the
door—a man with a black moustache walks in—turns to my
mother and says—"Miss Latour, will you marry me?" He
doesn't know she's pregnant.

CURTAIN

Scene Two

Scene is the same. Early the next morning.

*When the curtain rises again, daylight is streaming through the windows.
All doors closed. All curtains open.* MORTIMER *is still tied in his chair
and seems to be in a semi-conscious state.* JONATHAN *is asleep on sofa.*
EINSTEIN, *pleasantly intoxicated, is seated* L. *of table, his head resting on
table top.* O'HARA, *with his coat off and his collar loosened, is standing
over the stool which is between him and* MORTIMER. *He has progressed
to the most exciting scene of his play. There is a bottle of whisky and a
water tumbler on the table along with a plate full of cigarette butts.*

O'HARA. —there she is lying unconscious across the table in her
    lingerie—the chink is standing over her with a hatchet—(*he takes
    the pose*)—I'm tied up in a chair just like you are—the place is an
    inferno of flames—it's on fire—when all of a sudden—through
    the window—in comes Mayor LaGuardia. (EINSTEIN *raises his
    head and looks out the window. Not seeing anyone he reaches for the bottle
    and pours himself another drink.* O'HARA *crosses above to him and takes
    the bottle.*) Hey, remember who paid for that—go easy on it.

EINSTEIN. Vell, I'm listening, ain't I? (*He crosses to* JONATHAN *on the
    sofa.*)

O'HARA. How do you like it so far?

EINSTEIN. Vell, it put Chonny to sleep.

(O'HARA *has just finished a swig from the bottle.*)

O'HARA. Let him alone. If he ain't got no more interest than that—he don't get a drink. (EINSTEIN *takes his glass and sits on bottom stair. At the same time* O'HARA *crosses, puts stool under desk and whisky bottle on top of desk, then comes back to centre and goes on with his play* —) All right. It's three days later—I been transferred and I'm under charges—that's because somebody stole my badge. (*He pantomimes through following lines.*) All right. I'm walking my beat on Staten Island—forty-sixth precinct— when a guy I'm following, it turns out—is really following me. (*There is a knock on door.* EINSTEIN *goes up and looks out landing window. Leaves glass behind* D. S. *curtain.*) Don't let anybody in.—So I figure I'll outsmart him. There's a vacant house on the corner. I goes in.

EINSTEIN. It's cops!

O'HARA. I stands there in the dark and I see the door handle turn.

EINSTEIN (*rushing downstairs, shakes* JONATHAN *by the shoulder.*) Chonny! It's cops! Cops! (JONATHAN *doesn't move.* EINSTEIN *rushes upstairs and off through the arch.*)

(O'HARA *is going on with his story without a stop.*)

O'HARA. I pulls my guns—braces myself against the wall—and I says—"Come in." (OFFICERS BROPHY *and* KLEIN *walk in* R., *see* O'HARA *with gun pointed at them and raise their hands. Then, recognising their fellow officer, lower them.*) Hello, boys.

BROPHY. What the hell is going on here?

O'HARA (*goes to* BROPHY). Hey, Pat, whaddya know? This is Mortimer Brewster! He's going to write my play with me. I'm just tellin' him the story.

KLEIN (*crossing to* MORTIMER *and untying him*). Did you have to tie him up to make him listen?

BROPHY. Joe, you better report in at the station. The whole force is out looking for ya.

O'HARA. Did they send you here for me?

KLEIN. We didn't know you was here.

BROPHY. We came to warn the old ladies that there's hell to pay. The Colonel blew that bugle again in the middle of the night.

KLEIN. From the way the neighbours have been calling in about it you'd think the Germans had dropped a bomb on Flatbush Avenue. (*He has finished untying* MORTIMER. *Puts cords on sideboard.*)

BROPHY. The Lieutenant's on the warpath. He says the Colonel's got to be put away some place.

MORTIMER (*staggers to feet*). Yes! Yes!

O'HARA (*going to* MORTIMER). Gee, Mr. Brewster, I got to get away so I'll just run through the third act quick.

MORTIMER (*staggering* R.). Get away from me.

(BROPHY *gives* KLEIN *a look, goes to phone and dials.*)

KLEIN. Say, do you know what time it is? It's after eight o'clock in the morning.

O'HARA. It is? (*He follows* MORTIMER *to stairs.*) Gee, Mr. Brewster, them first two acts run a little long, but I don't see anything we can leave out.

MORTIMER (*almost to landing*). You can leave it *all* out.

(BROPHY *sees* JONATHAN *on sofa.*)

BROPHY. Who the hell is this guy?

MORTIMER (*hanging on railing, almost to balcony*). That's my brother.

BROPHY. Oh, the one that ran away? So he came back.

MORTIMER. Yes, he came back!

(JONATHAN *stirs as if to get up.*)

BROPHY (*into phone*). This is Brophy. Get me Mac. (*To* O'HARA, *sitting on bottom stair.*) I'd better let them know we found you, Joe. (*Into phone.*) Mac? Tell the Lieutenant he can call off the big manhunt—we got him. In the Brewster house. (JONATHAN *hears this and suddenly becomes very much awake, looking up to see* KLEIN *to* L. *of him and* BROPHY *to his* R.). Do you want us to bring him in? Oh—all right, we'll hold him right here. (*He hangs up.*) The Lieutenant's on his way over.

JONATHAN (*rising*). So I've been turned in, eh? (BROPHY *and* KLEIN *look at him with some interest.*) All right, you've got me! (*Turning to* MORTIMER, *who is on balcony looking down.*) And I suppose you and that stool-pigeon brother of mine will split the reward?

KLEIN. Reward?

(*Instinctively* KLEIN *and* BROPHY *both grab* JONATHAN *by an arm.*)

JONATHAN (*dragging Cops D. s. c.*). Now I'll do some turning in! You think my aunts are sweet charming old ladies, don't you? Well, there are thirteen bodies buried in the cellar.

MORTIMER (*as he rushes off to see* TEDDY). Teddy! Teddy! Teddy!

KLEIN. What the hell are you talking about?

BROPHY. You'd better be careful what you're saying about your aunts—they happen to be friends of ours.

JONATHAN (*raving as he drags them toward cellar door*). I'll show you! I'll prove it to you! You come to the cellar with me!

KLEIN. Wait a minute! Wait a minute!

JONATHAN. Thirteen bodies! I'll show you where they're buried.

KLEIN (*refusing to be kidded*). Oh, yeah?

JONATHAN. You don't want to see what's down in the cellar?

BROPHY (*releases* JONATHAN'S *arm, then to* KLEIN). Go on down in the cellar with him, Abe.

KLEIN (*drops* JONATHAN'S *arm backs* D. s. *a step and looks at him*). I'm not so sure I want to be down in the cellar with him. Look at that puss. He looks like Boris Karloff. (JONATHAN, *at mention of Karloff, grabs* KLEIN *by the throat, starts choking him.*) Hey—what the hell—Hey, Pat! Get him off me.

(BROPHY *takes out rubber blackjack.*)

BROPHY. Here, what do you think you're doing! (*He socks* JONATHAN *on head.* JONATHAN *falls unconscious, face down.*)

(KLEIN, *throwing* JONATHAN'S *weight to floor, backs away, rubbing his throat.*)

KLEIN. Well, what do you know about that?

(*There is a knock on door* R.)

O'HARA. Come in.

(LEIUTENANT ROONEY *bursts in* R., *slamming door after him. He is a very tough, driving, dominating officer.*)

ROONEY. What the hell are you men doing here? I told you I was going to handle this.

KLEIN. Well, sir, we was just about to—— (KLEIN's *eyes go to* JONATHAN *and* ROONEY *sees him.*)

ROONEY. What happened? Did he put up a fight?

BROPHY. This ain't the guy that blows the bugle. This is his brother. He tried to kill Klein.

KLEIN (*feeling his throat*). All I said was he looked like Boris Karloff.

ROONEY (*his face lights up*). Turn him over.

(*The two* COPS *turn* JONATHAN *over on his back.* KLEIN *steps back.* ROONEY *crosses front of* BROPHY *to take a look at* JONATHAN. BROPHY *drifts to* R. *of* ROONEY. O'HARA *is still at foot of stairs.*)

BROPHY. We kinda think he's wanted somewhere.

ROONEY. Oh, you kinda *think* he's wanted somewhere? If you guys don't look at the circulars we hang up in the station, at least you could read *True Detective.* (*Big.*) Certainly he's wanted. In Indiana! Escaped from the prison for the Criminal Insane! He's a lifer. For God's sake that's how he was described—he *looked* like Karloff!

KLEIN. Was there a reward mentioned?

ROONEY. Yeah—and *I'm* claiming it.

BROPHY. He was trying to get us down in the cellar.

KLEIN. He said there was thirteen bodies buried down there.

ROONEY (*suspicious*). Thirteen bodies buried in the cellar? (*Deciding it's ridiculous.*) And that didn't tip you off he came out of a nut-house!

O'HARA. I thought all along he talked kinda crazy.

(ROONEY *sees* O'HARA *for the first time. Turns to him.*)

ROONEY. Oh, it's Shakespeare! (*Crossing to him.*) Where have you been all night? And you needn't bother to tell me.

O'HARA. I've been right here, sir. Writing a play with Mortimer Brewster.

ROONEY (*tough*). Yeah? Well, you're gonna have plenty of time to write that play. You're suspended! Now get back and report in!

(O'HARA *takes his coat, night stick, and cap from top of desk. Goes to* R. *door and opens it. Then turns to* ROONEY.)

O'HARA. Can I come over some time and use the station typewriter?

ROONEY. No!—Get out of here. (O'HARA *runs out.* ROONEY *closes door and turns to the* COPS. TEDDY *enters on balcony and comes downstairs unnoticed and stands at* ROONEY'S *back to the* R. *of him.* ROONEY *to* COPS.) Take that guy somewhere else and bring him to. (*The* COPS *bend down to pick up* JONATHAN.) See what you can find out about his accomplice. (*The* COPS *stand up again in a questioning attitude.* ROONEY *explains.*) The guy that helped him escape. He's wanted too. No wonder Brooklyn's in the shape it's in, with the police force full of flatheads like you—falling for that kind of a story—thirteen bodies in the cellar!

TEDDY. But there are thirteen bodies in the cellar.

ROONEY (*turning on him*). Who are you?

TEDDY. I'm President Roosevelt.

(ROONEY *does a walk* U. S. *on this, then comes down again.*)

ROONEY. What the hell is this?

BROPHY. He's the fellow that blows the bugle.

KLEIN. Good morning, Colonel.

(*They salute* TEDDY, *who returns it.* ROONEY *finds himself saluting* TEDDY *also. He pulls his hand down in disgust.*)

ROONEY. Well, Colonel, you've blown your last bugle.

TEDDY (*seeing* JONATHAN *on floor*). Dear me—another Yellow Fever victim?

ROONEY. Whaat?

TEDDY. All the bodies in the cellar are Yellow Fever victims.

(ROONEY *crosses exasperatedly to* R. *door on this.*)

BROPHY. No, Colonel, this is a spy we caught in the White House.

ROONEY (*pointing to* JONATHAN). Will you get that guy out of here!

(COPS *pick up* JONATHAN *and drag him to kitchen.* TEDDY *follows them.* MORTIMER *enters, comes downstairs.*)

TEDDY (*turning back to* ROONEY). If there's any questioning of spies, that's my department!

ROONEY. You keep out of this!

TEDDY. You're forgetting! As President, I am also head of the Secret Service.

(BROPHY *and* KLEIN *exit with* JONATHAN *into kitchen.* TEDDY *follows them briskly.* MORTIMER *has come to* C.)

MORTIMER. Captain—I'm Mortimer Brewster.

ROONEY. Are you sure?

MORTIMER. I'd like to talk to you about my brother Teddy—the one who blew the bugle.

ROONEY. Mr. Brewster, we ain't going to talk about that—he's got to be put away!

MORTIMER. I quite agree with you. In fact, it's all arranged for. I had these commitment papers signed by Dr. Gilchrist, our family physician. Teddy has signed them himself, you see—and I've signed them as next of kin.

ROONEY. Where's he going?

MORTIMER. Happy Dale.

ROONEY. All right, I don't care where he goes as long as he goes!

MORTIMER. Oh, he's going all right. But I want you to know that everything that's happened around here Teddy's responsible for. Now, those thirteen bodies in the cellar——

ROONEY (*he's had enough of those thirteen*). Yeah—yeah—those thirteen bodies in the cellar! It ain't enough that the neighbours are all afraid of him, and his disturbing the peace with that bugle—but can you imagine what would happen if that cock-eyed story about thirteen bodies in the cellar got around? And now he's starting a Yellow Fever scare. Cute, ain't it?

MORTIMER (*greatly relieved, with an embarrassed laugh*). Thirteen bodies. Do you think anybody would believe that story?

ROONEY. Well, you can't tell. Some people are just dumb enough. You don't know what to believe sometimes. About a year ago a crazy guy starts a murder rumour over in Greenpoint, and I had to dig up a half acre lot, just to prove that——

(*There is a knock on* R. *door.*)

MORTIMER. Will you excuse me? (*He goes to door and admits* ELAINE *and* MR. WITHERSPOON, *an elderly, tight-lipped disciplinarian. He is carrying a brief case.*)

ELAINE (*briskly*). Good morning, Mortimer.

MORTIMER (*not knowing what to expect*). Good morning, dear.

ELAINE. This is Mr. Witherspoon. He's come to meet Teddy.

MORTIMER. To meet Teddy?

ELAINE. Mr. Witherspoon's the superintendent of Happy Dale.

MORTIMER (*eagerly*). Oh, come right in. (*They shake hands.* MORTIMER *indicates* ROONEY.) This is Captain——

ROONEY. *Lieutenant* Rooney. I'm glad you're here, Super, because you're taking him back with you to-day!

WITHERSPOON. Today? I didn't know that——

ELAINE (*cutting in*). Not today!

MORTIMER. Look, Elaine, I've got a lot of business to attend to, so you run along home and I'll call you up.

ELAINE. Nuts! (*She crosses to window-seat and sits.*)

WITHERSPOON. I had no idea it was this immediate.

ROONEY. The papers are all signed, he goes today!

(TEDDY *backs into room from kitchen, speaking sharply in the direction whence he's come.*)

TEDDY. Complete insubordination! You men will find out I'm no mollycoddle. (*He slams door and comes down to below table.*) When the President of the United States is treated like that—what's this country coming to?

ROONEY. There's your man, Super.

MORTIMER. Just a minute! (*He crosses to* TEDDY *and speaks to him as to a child.*) Mr. President, I have very good news for you. Your term of office is over.

TEDDY. Is this March the Fourth?

MORTIMER. Practically.

TEDDY (*thinking*). Let's see—OH!—Now I go on my hunting trip to Africa! Well I must get started immediately. (*He starts across the room and almost bumps into* WITHERSPOON *at* C. *He looks at him then steps back to* MORTIMER.) Is he trying to move into the White House before I've moved out?

MORTIMER. Who, Teddy?

TEDDY (*indicating* WITHERSPOON). Taft!

MORTIMER. This isn't Mr. Taft, Teddy. This is Mr. Witherspoon—he's to be your guide in Africa.

TEDDY (*shakes hands with* WITHERSPOON *enthusiastically*). Bully! Bully! I'll bring down my equipment. (*He crosses to stairs.* MARTHA *and* ABBY *have entered on balcony during last speech and are coming downstairs.*) When the safari comes, tell them to wait. (*As he passes the* AUNTS *on his way to landing, he shakes hands with each, without stopping his walk*). Goodbye, Aunt Abby. Goodbye Aunt Martha. I'm on my way to Africa—isn't it wonderful? (*He has reached the landing.*) CHARGE! (*He charges up the stairs and off.*)

(*The* AUNTS *are at foot of stairs.*)

MORTIMER (*crossing to* AUNTS). Good morning, darlings.

MARTHA. Oh, we have visitors.

MORTIMER. (*he indicates* ROONEY *at* C.). This is Lieutenant Rooney.

ABBY (*crossing, shakes hands with him*). How do you do, Lieutenant? My, you don't look like the fussbudget the policemen say you are.

MORTIMER. Why the Lieutenant is here—— You know, Teddy blew his bugle again last night.

MARTHA. Yes, we're going to speak to Teddy about that.

ROONEY. It's a little more serious than that, Miss Brewster.

MORTIMER (*easing* AUNTS *to* WITHERSPOON *who is above table where he has opened his brief case and extracted some papers.*) And you haven't met Mr. Witherspoon. He's the Superintendent of Happy Dale.

ABBY. Oh, Mr. Witherspoon—how do you do?

MARTHA. You've come to meet Teddy.

ROONEY (*somewhat harshly*). He's come to *take* him.

(*The* AUNTS *turn to* ROONEY *questioningly.*)

MORTIMER (*making it as easy as possible*). Aunties—the police want Teddy to go there, today.

ABBY (*crossing to* R. *of chair*). Oh—no!

MARTHA (*behind* ABBY). Not while we're alive!

ROONEY. I'm sorry, Miss Brewster, but it has to be done. The papers are all signed and he's going along with the Superintendent.

ABBY. We won't permit it. We'll promise to take the bugle away from him.

MARTHA. We won't be separated from Teddy.

ROONEY. I'm sorry, ladies, but the law's the law! He's committed himself and he's going!

ABBY. Well, if he goes, we're going too.

MARTHA. Yes, you'll have to take us with him.

MORTIMER (*has an idea. Crosses to* WITHERSPOON). Well, why not?

WITHERSPOON (*to* MORTIMER). Well, that's sweet of them to want to, but it's impossible. You see, we can't take *sane* people at Happy Dale.

MARTHA (*turning to* WITHERSPOON). Mr. Witherspoon, if you'll let us live there with Teddy, we'll see that Happy Dale is in our will—and for a very generous amount.

WITHERSPOON. Well, the Lord knows we could use the money, but—I'm afraid——

ROONEY. Now let's be sensible about this, ladies. For instance, here I am wasting my morning when I've got serious work to do. You know there are still *murders* to be solved in Brooklyn.

MORTIMER. Yes! (*Covering.*) Oh, are there?

ROONEY. It ain't only his bugle blowing and the neighbours all afraid of him, but things would just get worse. Sooner or later we'd be put to the trouble of digging up your cellar.

ABBY. Our cellar?

ROONEY. Yeah.—Your nephew's telling around that there are thirteen bodies buried in your cellar.

ABBY. But there are thirteen bodies in our cellar.

(ROONEY *looks disgusted.* MORTIMER *drifts quietly to front of cellar door.*)

MARTHA. If that's why you think Teddy has to go away—you come down to the cellar with us and we'll prove it to you. (*Goes* U. S.)

ABBY. There's one—Mr. Spenalzo—who doesn't belong here and who will have to leave—but the other twelve are our gentlemen. (*She starts* U. S.)

MORTIMER. I don't think the Lieutenant wants to go down in the cellar. He was telling me that only last year he had to dig up a half-acre lot—weren't you, Lieutenant?

ROONEY. That's right.

ABBY (*to* ROONEY). Oh you wouldn't have to dig here. The graves are all marked. We put flowers on them every Sunday.

ROONEY. Flowers? (*He steps up toward* ABBY, *then turns to* WITHERSPOON, *indicating the* AUNTS *as he speaks.*) Superintendent —don't you think you can find room for these ladies?

WITHERSPOON. Well, I——

ABBY (*to* ROONEY). You come along with us, and we'll show you the graves.

ROONEY. I'll take your word for it, lady—I'm a busy man. How about it, Super?

WITHERSPOON. Well, they'd have to be committed.

MORTIMER. Teddy committed himself. Can't they commit themselves? Can't they sign the papers?

WITHERSPOON. Why, certainly.

MARTHA (*sits in chair* L. *of table as* WITHERSPOON *draws it out for her*). Oh, if we can go with Teddy, we'll sign the papers. Where are they?

ABBY (*sitting* R. *of table.* MORTIMER *helps her with chair*). Yes, where are they?

(WITHERSPOON *opens brief case for more papers.* KLEIN *enters from kitchen.*)

KLEIN. He's coming around, Lieutenant.

ABBY. Good morning, Mr. Klein.

MARTHA. Good morning, Mr. Klein. Are you here too?

KLEIN. Yeah, Brophy and me have got your other nephew out in the kitchen.

ROONEY. Well, sign 'em up, Superintendent. I want to get this all cleaned up. (*He crosses to kitchen door, shaking his head as he exits and saying:*) Thirteen bodies.

(KLEIN *follows him out.* MORTIMER *is to the* L. *of* ABBY, *fountain pen in hand.* WITHERSPOON *to* R. *of* MARTHA, *also with pen.*)

WITHERSPOON (*handing* MARTHA *pen.*) If you'll sign right here.

(MARTHA *signs.*)

MORTIMER. And you here, Aunt Abby.

ABBY (*signing*). I'm really looking forward to going—the neighbourhood here has changed so.

MARTHA. Just think, a front lawn again.

(EINSTEIN *enters through arch and comes downstairs to door* D. R. *carrying suitcase. He picks hat from hall tree on way down.*)

WITHERSPOON. Oh, we're overlooking something.

MARTHA. What?

WITHERSPOON. Well, we're going to need the signature of a doctor.

MORTIMER. Oh! (*He sees* EINSTEIN *about to disappear through the door.*)
Dr. Einstein! Will you come over here—we'd like you to sign
some papers.

EINSTEIN. Please, I must——

MORTIMER (*crosses to him*). Just come right over, Doctor. At one
time last night, I thought the Doctor was going to operate on
me. (EINSTEIN *puts down suitcase and his hat just inside the door.*) Just
come right over, Doctor. (EINSTEIN *crosses to table,* L. *of* ABBY.)
Just sign right here, Doctor.

(*The* DOCTOR *signs* ABBY's *paper and* MARTHA's *paper.* ROONEY
and KLEIN *enter from kitchen.* ROONEY *crosses to desk and dials phone.*
KLEIN *stands near kitchen door.*)

ABBY. Were you leaving, Doctor?

EINSTEIN (*signing papers*). I think I must go.

MARTHA. Aren't you going to wait for Jonathan?

EINSTEIN. I don't think we're going to the same place.

(MORTIMER *sees* ELAINE *on window-seat and crosses to her.*)

MORTIMER. Hello, Elaine. I'm glad to see you. Stick around,
huh?

ELAINE. Don't worry, I'm going to.

(MORTIMER *stands back of* MARTHA's *chair.* ROONEY *speaks into
phone.*)

ROONEY. Hello, Mac. Rooney. We've picked up that guy that's
wanted in Indiana. Now there's a description of his
accomplice—it's right on the desk there—read it to me.
(EINSTEIN *sees* ROONEY *at phone. He starts toward kitchen and sees*
KLEIN *standing there. He comes back to* R. *of table and stands there
dejectedly waiting for the pinch.* ROONEY *repeats the description given
him over phone, looking blankly at* EINSTEIN *the while.*) Yeah—about
fifty-four—five foot six—hundred and forty pounds—blue
eyes—talks with a German accent. Poses as a doctor. Thanks,
Mac. (*He hangs up as* WITHERSPOON *crosses to him with papers in
hand.*)

WITHERSPOON. It's all right, Lieutenant. The Doctor here has just
completed the signatures.

(ROONEY *goes to* EINSTEIN *and shakes his hand.*)

ROONEY. Thanks, Doc. You're really doing Brooklyn a service. (ROONEY *and* KLEIN *exit to kitchen.*)

(EINSTEIN *stands amazed for a moment then grabs up his hat and suitcase and disappears through* R. *door. The* AUNTS *rise and cross over, looking out after him.* ABBY *shuts the door and they stand there* D. R.)

WITHERSPOON (*above table*). Mr. Brewster, you sign now as next of kin.

(*The* AUNTS *whisper to each other as* MORTIMER *signs.*)

MORTIMER. Yes, of course. Right here?

WITHERSPOON. That's fine.

MORTIMER. That makes everything complete—everything legal?

WITHERSPOON. Oh yes.

MORTIMER (*with relief*). Well, Aunties, now you're safe.

WITHERSPOON (*to* AUNTS). When do you think you'll be ready to start?

ABBY (*stepping* L.). Well, Mr. Witherspoon, why don't you go upstairs and tell Teddy just what he can take along?

WITHERSPOON. Upstairs?

MORTIMER. I'll show you.

ABBY (*stopping him*). No, Mortimer, you stay here. We want to talk to you. (*To* WITHERSPOON.) Yes, Mr. Witherspoon, just upstairs and turn to the left.

(WITHERSPOON *puts his brief case on sofa and goes upstairs, the* AUNTS *keeping an eye on him while talking to* MORTIMER.)

MARTHA. Well, Mortimer, now that we're moving, this house really is yours.

ABBY. Yes, dear, we want you to live here now.

MORTIMER (*below table*). No, Aunt Abby, this house is too full of memories.

MARTHA. But you'll need a home when you and Elaine are married.

MORTIMER. Darlings, that's very indefinite.

ELAINE (*rises and crosses to* L. *of* MORTIMER). It's nothing of the kind—we're going to be married right away.

(WITHERSPOON *has exited off balcony.*)

ABBY. Mortimer—Mortimer, we're really very worried about something.

MORTIMER. Now, darlings, you're going to love it at Happy Dale.

MARTHA. Oh, yes, we're very happy about the whole thing. That's just it—we don't want anything to go wrong.

ABBY. Will they investigate those signatures?

MORTIMER. Don't worry, they're not going to look up Dr. Einstein.

MARTHA. It's not his signature, dear, it's yours.

ABBY. You see, you signed as next of kin.

MORTIMER. Of course. Why not?

MARTHA. Well, dear, it's something we never wanted to tell you. But now you're a man—and it's something Elaine should know too. You see, dear—you're not really a Brewster.

(MORTIMER *stares as does* ELAINE.)

ABBY. Your mother came to us as a cook—and you were born about three months afterward.* But she was such a sweet woman—and such a good cook we didn't want to lose her—so brother married her.

MORTIMER. I'm—not—really—a—Brewster?

MARTHA. Now, don't feel badly about it, dear.

ABBY. And Elaine, it won't make any difference to you?

MORTIMER (*turning slowly to face* ELAINE. *His voice rising.*) Elaine! Did you hear? Do you understand? I'm a bastard!

---

* Directors who may wish to modify the situation mentioned by Abby may add the following to the text after the words "three months afterward": "... her poor husband had just died, and she was such," etc. Then add, "So we adopted the baby and brought him up ourselves." Mortimer's line "I'm a bastard" will, in this case, be omitted.

(ELAINE *leaps into his arms. The two* AUNTS *watch them, then* MARTHA *starts* U. L. *a few steps.*)

MARTHA. Well, now I really must see about breakfast.

ELAINE (*leading* MORTIMER *to* R. *door; opening door.*) Mortimer's coming over to my house. Father's gone to Philadelphia, and Mortimer and I are going to have breakfast together.

MORTIMER. Yes, I need some coffee—I've had quite a night.

ABBY. In that case I should think you'd want to get to bed.

MORTIMER (*with a sidelong glance at* ELAINE). I do. (*They exit* R., *closing door.*)

(WITHERSPOON *enters on balcony, carrying two canteens. He starts downstairs when* TEDDY *enters carrying large canoe paddle. He is dressed in Panama outfit with pack on his back.*)

TEDDY. One moment, Witherspoon. Take this with you! (*He exits off balcony again as* WITHERSPOON *comes on downstairs to sofa. He puts canteens on sofa and leans paddle against wall.*)

(*At the same time* ROONEY *and the two* COPS *with* JONATHAN *between them enter. The* COPS *have twisters around* JONATHAN'S *wrists.* ROONEY *enters first and crosses to* R. C. *The other three stop* D. L. *of table. The* AUNTS *are* R. *of the table.*)

ROONEY. We won't need the waggon. My car's out front.

MARTHA. Oh, you leaving now, Jonathan?

ROONEY. Yeah—he's going back to Indiana. There's some people there want to take care of him for the rest of his life. Come on. (ROONEY *opens door as the two* COPS *and* JONATHAN *cross to* R. C. ABBY *steps* D. S. *after they pass.*)

ABBY. Well, Jonathan, it's nice to know you have some place to go.

MARTHA. We're leaving too.

ABBY. Yes, we're going to Happy Dale.

JONATHAN. Then this house is seeing the last of the Brewsters.

MARTHA. Unless Mortimer wants to live here.

JONATHAN. I have a suggestion to make. Why don't you turn this property over to the church?

ABBY. Well, we never thought of that.

JONATHAN. After all, it *should* be part of the cemetery.

ROONEY. All right, get going, I'm a busy man.

JONATHAN (*holding his ground for his one last word*). Goodbye,
Aunties. Well, I can't better my record now, but neither can
you—at least I have that satisfaction. The score stands even,
twelve to *twelve*. (JONATHAN *and the* COPS *exit* R., *as the* AUNTS *look
out after them.*)

(WITHERSPOON *crosses above to window-seat and stands quietly looking
out the window. His back is to the* AUNTS.)

MARTHA (*starting toward* R. *door to close it*). Jonathan always was a
mean boy. Never could stand to see anyone get ahead of him.
(*She closes door.*)

ABBY (*turning slowly around* L. *as she speaks*). I wish we could show
him he isn't so smart! (*Her eyes fall on* WITHERSPOON. *She studies
him.* MARTHA *turns from door and sees* ABBY's *comtemplation.* ABBY
speaks sweetly.) Mr. Witherspoon? (WITHERSPOON *turns around
facing them.*) Does your family live with you at Happy Dale?

WITHERSPOON. I have no family.

ABBY. Oh——

MARTHA (*stepping into room*). Well, I suppose you consider every
one at Happy Dale your family?

WITHERSPOON. I'm afraid you don't quite understand. As head of
the institution, I have to keep quite aloof.

ABBY. That must make it very lonely for you.

WITHERSPOON. It does. But my duty is my duty.

ABBY (*turning to* MARTHA). Well, Martha—— (MARTHA *takes her
cue and goes to sideboard for bottle of wine. Bottle in* L. *cupboard is
empty. She puts it back and takes out full bottle from* R. *cupboard. She
brings bottle and wine-glass to table.* ABBY *continues talking.*) If Mr.
Witherspoon won't join us for breakfast, I think at least we
should offer him a glass of elderberry wine.

WITHERSPOON (*severely.*) Elderberry wine?

MARTHA. We make it ourselves.

WITHERSPOON (*melting slightly*). Why, yes . . . (*Severely again.*) Of course, at Happy Dale our relationship will be more formal—but here—— (*He sits in chair* L. *of table as* MARTHA *pours wine.* ABBY *is beside* MARTHA.) You don't see much elderberry wine nowadays—I thought I'd had my last glass of it.

ABBY. Oh, no——

MARTHA (*handing him glass of wine*). No, here it is.

(WITHERSPOON *toasts the ladies and lifts glass to his lips, but the curtain falls before he does* . . .)

(*For a curtain call it is suggested the twelve elderly gentlemen file out of the cellar entrance, stand in a line across stage, and bow.*)

THE END

PROPERTY PLOT

Act I.

On Stage.
Candles.
Two candelabra.
Tea things on table.
Tray—Abby.
Bundle of papers in desk drawer—Mortimer.
Cape and gloves on table—Martha.
Three goblets from left cupboard in sideboard.
Pepper and salt on sideboard—Martha.
Napkins and rings from left drawer in sideboard—Abby.
Water glass on table—Mortimer.
Bottle of wine and glass from cupboard—Abby.
Stationery in desk—Abby.
Matches on sideboard—Abby.

Off Stage.
Bugle—Teddy.
Covered pail—Abby.
Large cardboard box containing toy soldier—Teddy.
Brooch on dress—Martha.
Blue-backed legal paper—Dr. Harper.
Handbag containing mirror, etc.—Elaine.
Hat—Mortimer.
Dollar bills and papers—Mortimer.
Silencer (a pad that goes under tablecloth)—Abby.
Tablecloth—Abby.
Table silver and plates on tray—Martha.
Tray with plates, cups, saucers, etc.—Martha.
"Lazy Susan" (a sort of cruet for salt, pepper, sugar, etc.)—Martha.
Hat—Einstein.
Hat—Jonathan.
Flask—Einstein.

Act II.

On Stage.
Saucer on table.
Cigar—Jonathan.
Snapshot photo—Jonathan.
Dummy in window-seat—Teddy.

Off Stage.	Book and solar topee—Teddy.
	Pince-nez—Teddy.
	Flask—Einstein.
	Two dusty bags and large instrument case— Einstein.
	Matches—Jonathan and Einstein.
	Dummy body—Einstein and Jonathan.
	Handkerchief—Einstein.
	Suitcase and hat—Mortimer.
	Sports shoe belonging to Spenalzo.
	Bags—Einstein and Jonathan.
	Tray of coffee and sandwiches—Martha.

ACT III, SCENE I.

On Stage.	Hymnal and black gloves on sideboard—Abby.
	Hymnal and black gloves on table—Martha.
	Hat on hall tree—Mortimer.
	Curtain cords—Jonathan.
	Candelabra on sideboard.
	Bottle and two wine-glasses in left cupboard in sideboard.
Off Stage.	Bugle—Teddy.
	Legal paper—Mortimer.
	Instrument case containing surgical instruments, towel and rubber gloves—Jonathan.
	Penknife—Jonathan.
	Handkerchief—Einstein.
	Flask—Einstein.
	Large silk handkerchief—Jonathan.

ACT III, SCENE II.

On Stage.	Bottle of whisky and water.
	Tumbler on table.
	Plateful of cigarette butts on table.
	Fountain pen—-Mortimer.
	Pen—Martha.
	Bottle of wine in right cupboard of sideboard— Martha.
Off Stage.	Gun—O'Hara.
	Brief case including papers—Mr. Witherspoon.
	Suitcase—Einstein.
	Two canteens—Witherspoon.
	Large canoe paddle—Teddy.

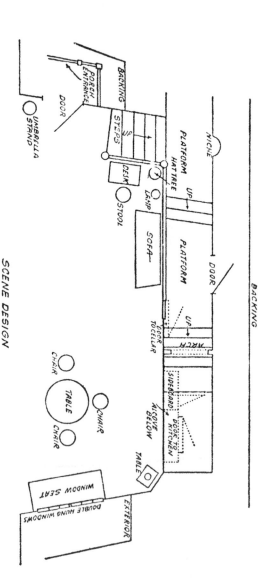

SCENE DESIGN
ARSENIC & OLD LACE